Government for the Third American Century

Government for the Third American Century

Donald L. Robinson
SMITH COLLEGE

Foreword by Lloyd N. Cutler, C. Douglas Dillon,
and Nancy Landon Kassebaum,
Committee on the Constitutional System

Westview Press
BOULDER, SAN FRANCISCO, & LONDON

Copyright © 1989 by the Committee on the Constitutional System

Published in 1989 in the United States of America by Westview Press, Inc., 5500 Central Avenue, Boulder, Colorado 80301, and in the United Kingdom by Westview Press, Inc., 13 Brunswick Centre, London WC1N 1AF, England

Library of Congress Cataloging-in-Publication Data
Robinson, Donald L., 1936–
  Government for the Third American Century/by Donald L.
Robinson.
    p. cm.
  Includes bibliographical references.
  ISBN 0-8133-0936-0. ISBN 0-8133-0935-2 (pbk.)
  1. United States—Politics and government—1945–   I. Title.
JK271.R5355 1989
320.973—dc20   89-36439
                                                                                   CIP

Printed and bound in the United States of America

The paper used in this publication meets the requirements of the American National Standard for Permanence of Paper for Printed Library Materials Z39.48-1984.

10   9   8   7   6   5   4   3   2   1

To my students at Smith College,
for demonstrating that citizens can recover
the ability to think constitutionally

Contents

Foreword

As the Constitution enters its third century, we are witnessing what appears to be a polar shift in how the constitutional system operates.

While the Constitution does not mention political parties, the framers promptly organized broadly based national parties in order to make the brave new system work. For most of our history the cohesive force of party loyalty usefully offset the centrifugal force of separate executive and legislative branches. The party that won the presidency also won a majority of both houses of Congress. In the second half of this century, however, voter loyalty to parties has declined. Now we usually elect a president of one party and a majority of the other party in one or both houses of Congress. In the resulting divided government, there is no counterforce to the centrifugal pull of the separate branches away from one another, and when we are governed poorly, neither party can fairly be held accountable.

The Committee on the Constitutional System was organized in 1982 as a nonpartisan, nonprofit organization of citizens concerned about this and other problems of national governance. Most of the members have served in either the Congress or the executive branch or both or have addressed the subject as scholars. Although not in full accord on the solutions to the problems of ineffective and unaccountable government, they are convinced that these problems demand widespread and intensive public discussion.

The Committee has sponsored two earlier books directed to this need. *Reforming American Government,* a compendium of basic papers on the strengths and weaknesses of our constitutional system, was edited by Professor Donald L. Robinson and published by Westview Press in 1985. *Constitutional Reform and Effective Government,* a detailed analysis and criticism of the government's institutional structure and of proposed remedies, by James L. Sundquist, was published by the Brookings Institution in 1986. And the Committee issued a summary report of its own conclusions and recommendations in 1987. (Copies of the 1987 report, entitled "A Bicentennial Analysis of the American Political Structure," are available from the Committee on the Constitutional System, Suite 410, 1755 Massachusetts Avenue NW, Washington, DC 20036.)

With the benefit of grants from the Ford, CBS, Rockefeller, Hewlett, MacArthur, and American Express foundations and the Dillon Fund, and with additional support from our members, 10,000 copies of each of these works have been distributed throughout the country and discussed in twenty regional gatherings as well as in the Committee's regular meetings in Washington.

Those discussions have indicated the need to update the presentation of the problem and potential solutions in a pro-and-con format designed to encourage broad debate and understanding. A further grant from the Dillon Fund has made this possible, and we are very pleased that Professor Robinson has taken on this new challenge.

The 1988 vote has once again (for the fifth time in the last six presidential elections) given the country a divided government. Looking ahead, the Committee has asked Lloyd Cutler and James Sundquist to join with other scholars and practitioners in examining the consequences of divided government during the first year of the Bush administration. A basic premise of the resulting coedited volume is that the nation must either find new institutional approaches and devices for making divided government work or devise reforms to reduce the risk of its recurrence. Westview will publish the work in the fall of 1990 as a companion to the present volume.

This sequence will bring needed attention to a profound public question: Can our government perform adequately in the third century of our national life?

Lloyd N. Cutler
C. Douglas Dillon
Nancy Landon Kassebaum
Co-Chairs
Committee on the Constitutional System

Preface

This book is a primer for debate about the fitness of the American political system as it moves toward the twenty-first century. It focuses on structural matters: the electoral process, the major institutions of the federal government and how they interact, and what we can do when they perform ineffectively or abuse their powers. This focus on structure has led us to exclude certain topics that come to mind when people discuss "constitutional reform." We do not, for example, consider an amendment to allow prayer in school or ban abortions. These are important questions, but they do not affect the structure of the government directly. They will be accomplished or blocked by the existing machinery. Nor do we devote attention to the judiciary. This choice is perhaps harder to justify, given our focus on institutions and their interactions. Our reasoning is that the courts are functioning well enough at the moment. The threats to the viability of our system in the twenty-first century arise not from the judiciary but from the political system. Nor do we address the federal system: questions of the distribution of functions between the federal and state governments. Again, these are important questions, and in this case they certainly do affect the structure of constitutional government. But they are separate from the focus I have chosen.

The Introduction (Chapter 1) notes that the framers set the example for bold action on structural reform and continued to innovate, even after the Constitution was ratified and put in operation. In fact, structural innovation has been an ongoing tradition in America.

Part 1 presents a survey of recent developments in three areas that arouse deep concern among political leaders, scholars, and ordinary citizens. Because we are, most fundamentally, a constitutional democracy, we turn first to the electoral system. Americans have always scorned politicians and heaped ridicule on the humbug of political campaigns. Recently, however, for many voters distaste has turned to disgust and finally to cynicism and apathy. In Chapter 2, we analyze these developments and relate them to the decline of our political parties. Next (Chapter 3), we look at the recent performance of the government as manager of a modern, national economy. We try to penetrate the political rhetoric that surrounds economic issues and to determine whether the structure of government has contributed to our difficulties in this area. The survey concludes in Chapter 4 with the troubled story of foreign relations and control of the war powers since World War II.

Part 2 begins the debate over the need for basic reform of the American political system. In Chapter 5, we present one side of the argument: the contention that structural reforms, including constitutional amendments, are necessary to preserve effective, accountable government into the twenty-first century. In Chapter 6, we outline the rebuttal: the argument that the flexibility and adaptability of the American system have been amply demonstrated over the past two hundred years and that the framers' Constitution embodies wisdom that we dare not abandon in these troubled times.

Part 3 proceeds on the assumption that structural reforms are at least worth considering. It presents a dozen separate proposals, under three headings: How We Choose Our Leaders; How Government Works Together; and What We Do When Government Fails.

The format for each proposal discussed in Part 3 is the same. We begin with a statement of "The Existing Situation," outlining the provisions of the Constitution and laws on the issue in question. Next, to frame the debate, we present "The Basic Proposal" in the form of a resolution that advocates the reform in question. We briefly discuss the implications of the resolution and, in some cases, show how the reform in question can be modified in various ways. The next section, called "Relevant Facts," gives the necessary background for considering each proposal. The core of each presentation is a pair of sections that outline the case for and against the proposed change. A concluding section ("You Decide") puts two or three questions that drive toward a decision on the resolution.

In Part 3, we look at electoral changes first, because the effective use of the ballot is fundamental to a democracy. Chapter 7 presents a discussion of six proposals to reform the electoral system. The first is a change in the length of terms for members of Congress, a constitutional amendment put forward in various forms through the years by many political leaders, including President Lyndon Johnson. The second is a device that could probably be put in place by federal statute: allowing voters in all federal elections to vote for a "team ticket," thereby casting a ballot for all candidates nominated by a given party. The third and fourth proposals are designed to reform campaign finance: one (requiring a constitutional amendment) would put a cap on campaign spending; the other (by statute or party rules) would provide public funds for television broadcasting of candidates' appeals. The fifth (requiring a constitutional amendment) is a proposal to eliminate the electoral college and provide for the direct election of presidents. The sixth and final proposal in this section (also requiring an amendment) would eliminate the office of vice-president and otherwise provide for succession to the presidency.

In Chapter 8, we consider four suggestions for improving the interaction of the government's parts. The first two proposals would enable the president (by constitutional amendment) to select members of Congress for his or her cabinet and clear the way for the president (by informal agreement) to appear regularly before Congress to answer questions about the administration's policies and actions. The final two proposals discuss methods of revising the War Powers Resolution and compelling a balanced budget.

Chapter 9 turns to measures for coping with stalemates and breakdowns—when the system functions so badly that we need to resort to extraordinary procedures. The first would incorporate into the Constitution, by amendment, a means of dissolving the government and holding new elections before the full terms of office have expired. The other would introduce, by amendment, a means of enacting legislation by national referendum.

Chapter 10 concludes this series by asking whether reforms, if we want them at all, should be considered each on its own merits, one by one, or in packages. The Constitution is a complicated, delicately balanced whole. Changing one aspect will influence others. To achieve the desired effect and to keep the system balanced, we may wish to consider reforms in combination.

Part 4 accepts as its premise the idea that reforms are needed and asks how to proceed. Continuing with the pro-and-con format, Chapter 11 debates the merits of the traditional method of amending the Constitution (originating in Congress) versus the approach that originates in the states and proceeds to a national convention.

The book concludes with the text of the Constitution, Suggestions for Further Reading, and a listing of current members of the Board of Directors of the Committee on the Constitutional System.

Donald L. Robinson
Ashfield, Massachusetts

Acknowledgments

I have had a great deal of help in writing this book. The idea was initiated at a meeting in Washington in June 1988 by a group of people associated with the Committee on the Constitutional System. The anxieties of the American people about the condition of the political system, deepened by the Iran-contra affair, were already being inundated in the maelstrom of the presidential campaign. Those present at the June meeting anticipated that these concerns would resurface by late 1989, once the honeymoon of the new administration was over and the government began to settle into its familiar pattern of stalemate and evasion of difficult issues. Present at that meeting were Douglas Dillon, Lloyd Cutler, David Bartel (representing Senator Nancy Kassebaum), Jim Sundquist, Jim Burns, Douglass Cater, Henry Reuss, Dot Ridings, Steve Charnovitz, Susan McCone, Mary and Peter Schauffler, and a few others. We all agreed on the need for a "debate book," outlining the issues and providing materials for a thorough discussion of various reforms. The goal would be to equip a wider array of citizens to enter into discussions that were already attracting a good deal of attention among leaders of the Washington political community. I agreed to attempt such a volume. As the work progressed, I continued to have the valuable assistance of Messrs. Dillon, Cutler, Sundquist, Burns, and Schauffler. Particularly in light of this kind help, I must emphasize that the selection of items to discuss, the priority they are given, and all aspects of the way they are treated in this book represent judgments that I alone have made.

I especially want to thank Messrs. Dillon and Cutler and Senator Kassebaum for their encouragement and support of this project. For the decade of our association, they have always made plain their commitment to the widest possible investigation of alternatives. By their stature, they have lent legitimacy to such inquiries. When the history of these years of constitutional government in the United States is written, these three leaders will be honored for keeping alive the belief that Americans do not have to accept things as they are, that we can admit the possibility that our ills are rooted in the structure of institutions, and that we can improve the performance of our political system.

Besides the continuing support and assistance of this group of friends in and around Washington, I have had other vital assistance. My principal community of learning for the past twenty years has consisted of students, colleagues, and alumnae of Smith College. I also want to thank Shep Forman, Charles Blitzer, and Fred and Ruth Friendly, again, for giving me opportunities to develop and present these ideas. As a visiting scholar for the Phi Beta Kappa Society this past academic year, I have had the privilege of sharing my thoughts with colleagues and students on several other campuses. The confidence and professionalism of Miriam Gilbert and Jennifer Knerr at Westview Press have also been of inestimable value.

I could not have completed the work on time without the help of Wendy Anderson. Word-processing reduces an author's need for a typist, but the author of a book like this still needs research assistance. He is doubly blessed if his assistant has an unblinking eye for awkward prose, combined with a kind heart and an unflappable temperament. And he has a treasure if his assistant is also adept with the issues involved in the study and is able to make valuable suggestions about the organization of the argument. Ms. Anderson will continue her studies next year at the Law School of the University of Virginia. I shall miss her sorely.

Ms. Anderson and I have had valuable assistance from Joan Mulloney and Djuna Perkins, who helped with research and proofreading. Janice Daily and others on the staff of Neilson Library at Smith College guided us to published materials.

On a personal level, the sacrifices demanded by this project were borne most heavily, and with unfailing sweetness and courage, by my dear wife, Molly.

For errors and misjudgments that have survived all these good efforts, I alone am responsible.

D.L.R.

1
Introduction: Government from Reflection and Choice

Two centuries ago Alexander Hamilton, a leader of the drive for political reform in America, persuaded New Yorkers that the Constitution was worth a try. It was not perfect, he admitted, but its basic principles were sound. Above all, it would hold the Union together. Besides, he said, as experience revealed its flaws, we could amend it.[1]

Hamilton's practical wisdom was deeply American. The important thing was to stick together and to embrace our common commitment to independence, liberty and government by consent of the governed. The means we could work out and adjust as problems developed.

The founders themselves did not hesitate to alter the system of government which they had created. When the people refused to accept their assurances that the national government would respect civil liberties, they quickly drew up a Bill of Rights and added it to the Constitution. When the electoral college misfired in the election of 1800, they added the Twelfth Amendment, specifying separate votes for president and vice-president.

Reform during the founding generation came in other ways, too, besides constitutional amendments. When political leaders felt frustrated as their programs faced defeat in Congress, they overcame their prejudice against "factions" and formed political parties that bridged the separation of powers.

Subsequent generations made further changes, some of them absolutely fundamental. The Civil War generation abolished slavery and established that no person could be denied the right to vote on account of race. Progressives around the turn of the century fought for, and eventually won, the direct election of senators and suffrage for women. It took monumental efforts to accomplish these reforms, but the nation was determined to learn from its experience and to improve the system inherited from the founders.

Again, some of the most significant changes occurred without amending the Constitution at all. President Andrew Jackson and his allies developed the national party convention for nominating presidential candidates. Later in the century, as railroads crossed state lines and conditions in the marketplace became too complex and changed too rapidly for Congress to regulate them by statute, legislators created the Interstate Commerce Commission. The Constitution provided separate branches of government to perform different functions, but here was a body that made rules, enforced them and settled disputes about them, all by itself.

In the twentieth century, Congress began to use the I.C.C. model for many other problems: to regulate stock markets, to license radio and television stations, to protect the right of working people to organize into trade unions, and to keep watch over elections. Many citizens were troubled by this development, which appeared to violate the spirit of the constitutional separation of powers, and the Supreme Court heard several cases that challenged one or another of these agencies. But the Court decided that they did not conflict with the constitutional provisions. As long as the commissioners were appointed in the usual way (by the president, with Senate confirmation), and as long as Congress retained the power to set the framework for the agencies, and to amend the guidelines at its discretion, the Court thought they represented a permissible adaptation of the Constitution to modern demands.

The evolution of constitutional form has continued to our own time. A recent example is the special prosecutor. Traditionally, it has been one of the principal responsibilities of the executive branch to conduct investigations and prosecute people suspected of engaging in criminal acts. In the aftermath of the Watergate scandals, however, people began to mistrust the executive branch itself. Could a president's top aides be trusted to prosecute themselves? The Constitution expects voters to punish a corrupt administration, but the election of 1972 convinced many people that a president involved in corruption could distort the political process to an extent that threatened the integrity of the whole system. Congress decided that the situation called for innovative measures. In 1978 it adopted the Ethics in Government Act. In the event that the Attorney General found any member of the executive branch (including himself) plausibly accused of serious crimes, the act bound him to ask a panel of judges to name a special prosecutor, independent of the Justice Department, with full power to investigate the charges and, if he or she deemed them sufficiently serious, to prosecute the officials in court.

There is no doubt that this procedure departs from the framers' design. Yet the Supreme Court has endorsed it, apparently convinced that experience in recent years justifies it.

What these developments show is that (as John Gardner has pointed out) a living nation is not a finished monument. The pharoahs built the pyramids, and they are still standing. We admire them, and we do our best to preserve them exactly as they were built. The pharoahs also built a form of government, but that has long since perished, because it could not adapt to changing demands.

A nation lives by the continuing efforts of a caring, believing people. Americans are united by a love for this land and by the challenge of creating a nation from the diverse people who have made their way here from all over the globe. (I include, of course, the so-called "native Americans," who came here earlier.) We are not of one "blood." Our national identity is bound up with the notion of *becoming* a people, by blending many racial and ethnic strains.

We are also united by the Constitution. We are a people of the covenant. The Constitution is our deepest bond. It is almost unthinkable for us to consider abandoning it or exchanging it for another model. It is far more than a mere form of government. It is the bedrock of our legitimacy as a nation.

At the same time, we are a practical people, and we are not afraid to consider our faults. That is why our political system has lasted for two centuries. We adhere to it, but not rigidly.

Our system has been under great strain recently. Many of the problems we confront seem to be rooted in the system itself. This book explores those problems and attempts to discern whether they arise from the usual stuff of politics (ignorance, haste, mischief, the clash of personalities), or from the tendency of the existing system to misdirect our efforts to govern ourselves fairly and effectively.

In testimony in 1982 before a congressional committee called to consider political reform, James MacGregor Burns offered two reasons for thinking boldly about such questions. "First," he said,

> there may well be—in the tumultuous century that lies ahead of us, there undoubtedly will be—a series of national and worldwide crises in which the capacity of our system will be so sorely tested that many Americans—perhaps rather suddenly—will feel an urgent need for change. It's very important, if we come to a point of great debate in this country over alternative systems, that we have done our homework, that we have

in our intellectual bank the kinds of ideas, the kind of analysis . . . that I think will come out of these hearings.

And second, we have had to learn in this century that it's almost always the impossible and the unpredictable that do happen. We, you and I, in our early years, could not possibly, I think, have imagined the kinds of incredible developments, both benign and malign, that have taken place in the past fifty years. So again, it seems to me that to consider the systemic changes is a matter of hard-headed practicality and not simply a kind of dreamy investigation.[2]

I would add to Professor Burns's admirable apologia for efforts of this kind just one other point. Like him, I am a college professor. Besides working with my own students, I spend a lot of time with high school teachers, developing materials to bring to life the teaching of the Constitution. We teachers find that the exploration of alternatives is an excellent way to engage students in the study of the American system. The results are unpredictable. Some students are impressed when they learn how other systems work and come to believe that ours would work better if we adopted some feature of another system. Others are confirmed in the conviction that the framers' system is sound and ought not to be changed. But in almost every case, their understanding and appreciation of the American system gains immeasurably.

Let us begin, then, with a survey of developments that lead many Americans to conclude that it is time for a thorough review of the operation of our political system, and time also to give careful consideration to proposals for reform.

PART ONE

SIGNS OF STRAIN
The Performance of the American System, 1950–1990

2
Choosing Leaders

We gauge the effectiveness of a constitutional system by the fruits of its governance. Is the nation safe from its enemies? Are its homes and streets and parks secure? Are its citizens productively and gainfully employed?

It is sometimes said that such criteria as these constitute the "bottom line" for a government. But for the United States, there is a bottom line *below* the bottom line. We justified our struggle for independent nationhood by the proposition that all men are created equal, and we dedicated ourselves to the quest for self-government, government "of the people, by the people, for the people." How close are we to achieving genuine self-government? Are citizens actively engaged in the political life of the nation? Is the government truly rooted in the popular will?

These questions draw attention to the electoral system, and it is to this topic that we turn first in this assessment of the health of the American constitutional system as it faces its third century.

Recent Concerns About the Electoral Process

We cannot deny that the electoral process has been a disappointing spectacle in recent years. Campaigns seem far too long, too costly, and too often uninformative, if not downright misleading. Not surprisingly, the response of voters, measured in terms of the number that turns out to vote on Election Day, has been declining, to the point that only half of the voting-age population cast a ballot for president in 1988.

Let us examine these concerns in a bit more detail.

Length of the Campaign. It is understandable, perhaps, that candidates and their aides often begin quietly to lay the groundwork many years before officially announcing their intention to run. But if the public phase of the presidential campaign of 1988 can be said to have started with the televised debates that both parties held in Texas in July, 1987, then it lasted a full sixteen months. Is this not too long a time? The public phase of campaigns in the other democracies lasts only a matter of weeks—three weeks in England, four or five in Canada.

Stephen Hess has argued that the presidential campaign in America is probably not longer than it needs to be.[1] Ronald Reagan and Michael Dukakis had been governors of their states, but their characters and records were not well known nationally before their campaigns for the presidency. We live in an age when rank-and-file voters, in primaries, choose their parties' nominees. Such voters may need a long season of primaries, as well as a long general campaign, to make a proper assessment of such candidates.

But the length of campaigns need not be tailored to the needs created by such candidates. Is it healthy for the affairs of the country to be held in suspension for such a long campaign?

Cost. The cost of modern elections, too, concerns many citizens. Senator Nancy Kassebaum (Republican, Kansas), co-chair of the Committee on the Constitutional System, notes that fund-raising for campaigns is "one of the most deadening and demeaning requirements of public office today." Voters see their representatives in Congress taking large sums of money from interest groups, sometimes from groups that have no involvement with affairs in the member's district, and it "erodes the confidence and trust that are the foundation of democracy." Senator Kassebaum admits to having "serious problems" with the idea of public financing of all federal campaigns, but she warns that we cannot afford to be complacent about the fact that a House race often costs $1 million and a Senate race up to twenty times as much. She concludes her remarks with a blunt warning:

> If government becomes a captive pawn of the well-heeled moneyman and the sharp media adviser, it will no longer be the champion of the average citizen. At that point, average citizens will have a lot to say about this matter, and they won't require large sums of money to deliver their message.[2]

Quality of Debate. We worry also about the poor quality of dialogue between candidates in political campaigns. So many of our impressions come from television advertising. These brief, repetitious messages are crafted by highly paid media specialists, who shape the images of their clients to the findings of public-opinion surveys. In addition, many seem deliberately negative, more designed to arouse mistrust of an opponent than to clarify the strengths of the sponsoring candidate.

The heralded "debates" between candidates promise a more revealing glimpse of their views and personalities, but by the time their handlers have finished setting the ground rules (concerning the number and timing of the encounters, the identity of the questioners, the format, and so on), any opportunity for true spontaneity has been reduced to a minimum. Again, the entire process is controlled by the candidates and their staffs, and it serves their interests, not the voters'.

Turnout. As we have noted, in the presential election of 1988, only about 50 percent of Americans old enough to vote cast ballots. Turnout for off-year congressional elections is even lower: about 39 percent in 1982 and 1986.

Turnout for the 1988 presidential election was the lowest since the elections of 1920 and 1924. In those earlier contests, the ranks of non-voters had been suddenly swelled by the addition of women, whose right to vote had just been guaranteed by the Nineteenth Amendment (ratified in August, 1920). It took time for these new voters to develop the habit of participation. By 1928, turnout had risen to 57 percent.

In the period since World War II, the peak of participation was in 1960, when it stood at 64 percent. Since then, there has been a steady decline, despite the removal of several barriers to voting (the elimination of the poll tax, more energetic enforcement of voting-rights laws in the southern states, the easing of residency requirements, and the introduction of postcard and Election Day registration in some states). In addition, other factors should have encouraged higher rates of turnout. Research shows that the more education a citizen has, the more likely he or she is to vote. But in recent years in America, voter turnout has continued to decline even though education levels have risen markedly.[3]

Turnout levels in America compare quite unfavorably with those in other democratic countries. In national elections between 1945 and 1980, the average turnout was 95 percent in Australia and the Netherlands, 87 percent in West Germany, 77 percent in Great Britain, 76 percent in Canada, and 73 percent Japan—but only 59 percent in the United States.[4] To interpret this data properly, one must bear in mind that foreign countries tend to calculate turnout as a percentage of *registered voters,* whereas we in America use *voting-age population* as the basis. To see the effect of this difference, consider the 1980 election. According to the 1980 Census, there were 164 million Americans of voting age. In the presidential election that year, 86.5 million valid ballots were cast, producing a turnout figure (as we calculate it) of 53 percent. But only 105 million Americans were registered to vote

that year. Thus, among those who were registered, 82 percent voted—
an excellent turnout, by the standards of other democracies.

Still, the questions remain: why are so many Americans (59 million
in 1980) not registered to vote, and would they vote if they were
registered?

There are many reasons for people not being registered to vote.
Some are not legally qualified. In 1980 there were about 9 million
resident aliens, who lack the citizenship required to vote. Also included
in the Census totals for voting-age population are "institutionalized"
persons, such as jailed felons and inmates of mental facilities; most
states do not allow such people to vote.

Even after discounting for these reasonable disqualifications, however,
there are tens of millions of Americans who are fully qualified to vote,
but still do not register. In most European countries, registration is
the government's responsibility. Some Americans have proposed that
we adopt a similar system. Citizens could be registered to vote automatically when they register a vehicle, or it could be tied somehow
to social security.

Some such strategy would doubtless have a marginal effect in boosting
turnout. However, most careful students of the problem of declining
participation have concluded, as Curtis Gans does, that "the answer
. . . does not lie in more sophisticated registration drives or new voting
laws—although universal registration, more polling places, shorter
ballots, fewer elections and better voter information would certainly
marginally increase turnout." It lies instead in "more fundamental"
factors, such as reversing "the decay of political and social institutions,
most notably the political party. . . ."[5]

Parties and American Political Development

It was not always thus. There was a time, in the last quarter of the
nineteenth century, when the turnout of eligible voters in America was
substantially higher than it is today: well over 75 percent for presidential
elections.[6] National elections during that period were often very close,
and control over Congress and the presidency shifted back and forth
between the parties. There was very little ticket-splitting, and feelings
of party loyalty were intense in most regions of the country. The
outcome of elections tended to turn on the ability of each party
organization to mobilize its own faithful supporters and deliver them
to the polls.

It was also—some would say, not coincidentally—a time of widespread
political corruption. Party bosses controlled nominations, and they used
patronage to reward the faithful and enforce discipline. The result,

many thought, was a debasement of the public service, in both its elective and appointive aspects.

Progressive reformers fiercely criticized these practices. Gradually their demands for change grew to a strong political force. One of their early triumphs came in the area of ballot reform. Through most of the nineteenth century, ballots were prepared by the parties. Voters went to their parties' headquarters and got a "ticket," then went to the polling place and deposited it, thereby casting a ballot for each of the parties' nominees. Under this system, one's political allegiances tended to become known to one's neighbors. In addition, most newspapers at that time had a strong party affiliation. Thus, one tended to learn about politics from partisan sources and to be reinforced in one's preferences.

Around the turn of the century, reformers gained a significant victory against this system: the introduction of the secret ballot, prepared and administered by the government. It listed all qualified candidates, thus encouraging voters who wished to "split their ticket." This reform, by itself, did not change ingrained habits of party loyalty, but it opened the way for greater independence in voting.

Other reforms soon followed. One was aimed at the link between state legislatures and federal patronage, via the United States Senate. To get elected to the Senate in those days, one had to have the support of the prevailing party in the state legislature, because the Constitution provided for senators to be chosen by state legislatures. One campaigned for the Senate in part by campaigning on behalf of one's fellow-partisans running for the state legislature. Meanwhile, everyone had an eye on federal patronage, because once elected, senators had a major role to play in the distribution of federal patronage.

In this atmosphere, reports abounded that senatorial elections often involved corrupt deals: State legislators voting for a Senate candidate in return for consideration on a federal job or contract. Reformers insisted that the only way to sever these shady connections was for the people to elect senators directly. In 1913, strong resistance in the Senate was finally overwhelmed, and the Seventeenth Amendment was speedily ratified. One result was a weakening of the partisan ties that bound senators to other politicians in their states.

Another target of reformers was the control of party bosses over nominations. To return control to the people, reformers insisted on the introduction of primary elections, to enable rank-and-file voters to choose the candidates that would square off in the general election. Sometimes the reformers went so far as to insist that a party's primary election must be open to all voters, not just those who were affiliated with the party. The use of primaries was spotty, and in many cases they were only advisory. Still, they gave expression to the suspicion that party leaders served their own interests, rather than the general public good, and they weakened the control of the party organizations over the electoral process.

These progressive reforms fed on the deep bias in American culture against political power belonging to any small group. No one thought very much about whose opportunities would be enhanced as the power of party leaders waned. The secret ballot, for example, strengthened those who preferred to conceal their partisan preferences: the so-called "independents." Independents are not randomly distributed across the socio-economic spectrum; they tend to be wealthier and better educated than the average voter. The other major reform, the move to primaries, favored those who were most likely to vote in these less publicized elections and improved the chances of candidates who excelled in direct appeals to voters, at the expense of those who could impress party leaders.

The impact of these changes on the national political system and on state laws was potentially enormous. However, in terms of the incidence of ticket-splitting and the control of parties over the governing process, they seem not to have made much difference through the first half of the twentieth century.[7] What finally did give impetus to the drive against party organizations as major players in electoral politics was the development of a constellation of modern technologies that revolutionized political life.

Perhaps the most powerful force for change was television.[8] Since mid-century, television has greatly affected the electoral process, changing the types of candidates who run well in modern campaigns and reducing the value of intermediaries between the candidate and the electorate, especially party organizations.

The ready availability of jet airplanes had a similar effect in weakening a candidate's dependence on party organization. No longer did someone running for president, or for senator in a large state, have to depend on party officials to carry a message to voters. He or she could deliver it in person, or by means of electronic media. Also, candidates no longer had to depend on party organizations to tell them what voters were thinking about. Opinion-gathering was professionalized. With the assistance of computers, these professionals could put a candidate in touch with sympathetic voters, targeting them for calls by phone banks or for computerized mailings.

All of this costs money, of course, and candidates can no longer depend on parties to raise the enormous funds that modern campaigning requires. At the nomination stage, parties cannot favor one candidate above another, so each candidate must build a personal organization.

Even during the general election, a candidate cannot expect to raise a very large proportion of needed funds from the party organization.

With the addition of these technological factors since mid-century, the potential of the Progressive reforms to loosen the hold of the parties has finally been realized. The electoral process encourages voters to be independent of any party, and party organization is no longer essential to candidates, either.

The result is that parties, having been deprived of their traditional functions, are no longer able to bind the system together as they once did. The American constitutional system tends to fragment power in two ways. It separates executive from legislative power. And it separates candidates from officials in office.

This latter point is less familiar than the one about separation of powers, but no less crucial to the role that parties have traditionally played in constitutional democracies. In order for elections to serve effectively as the link between voters and officials in office, there must be continuity between what a candidate promises in a campaign and what he or she does in office. Parties can help to forge those links. If an official wins office because his party chose him as its nominee and because he carried the party's banner in the campaign, he is obliged to honor that party's agenda in office. Once in office, if he strays from his party's commitments, its leaders can remind him of his responsibility to the party that nominated him and to the party's legions who campaigned and voted for him. Without these ties, he is free to do anything he can get away with; his ties to the constituency are unmediated by any organizational structure.

The Residual Strength of Parties

Not everyone agrees that parties are weaker than they used to be. The evidence of a weakening in partisanship among voters is clear,[9] but organizationally the national parties appear to have strengthened themselves considerably in recent years. Each national committee has a handsome, permanent headquarters building in Washington, D.C., staffed by professionals who are skilled at media relations, fund-raising, candidate recruitment and training, electoral law (a complicated field!), and all the other arts that are essential to success in the modern political arena. These marks of organizational stability and usefulness did not exist as recently as two decades ago.

In addition, further contributing to a possible resurgence of national parties, there has been a shift in partisanship nationally, a realignment of forces between the two parties. The biggest change is in the South, where Republicans have made great gains among conservative, white voters. Democrats, meanwhile, have made inroads among more liberal, suburban white voters in the Northeast and West.[10] These massive shifts alter the character of each party's coalition of electoral support. They ought in time to make it possible for parties to draft stronger platforms and perhaps to move with less resistance toward enforcing them on officials who bear the party label.

The Importance of Political Parties

In considering the value of parties in the political life of this country, we need to weigh several factors. Lloyd Cutler summarizes a number of them in a set of propositions he addresses to the question: "Should we try to rebuild party cohesion and party government?"

- Party government and party cohesion are not anachronisms in modern democratic societies. They exist in most of the other industrial democracies and in many of our own states. The fact that they flourish in these other democracies and in our own state governments is strong evidence that their recent decline in our national government is neither inevitable nor irreversible.
- Our national government today has many more major decisions to make today than ever before. The competing interests involved in each decision are far more complex. We hold government responsible today not merely for the goals set forth in the preamble of the Constitution—to establish justice, insure domestic tranquility and provide for the national defense—but also for the macro-management of the national and world economy and the defense of the entire free world. Even conservative incumbents now accept this broad mandate.
- Because of the growing interdependence between our national economy, national security and domestic tranquility and the economy, security and tranquility of other nations, many of the decisions our government must make involve reaching and keeping agreements with other governments.
- Without party cohesion and party government, it is extraordinarily difficult to make major domestic decisions and agreements with other governments, because each decision depends on forming a different cross-party coalition.
- Without party cohesion and party government, both parties and their elected officials usually condemn the resulting hodgepodge of outcomes, yet manage to avoid being held accountable for them. As we have seen, the ability of incumbents of both parties to shift the blame and win reelection has been phenomenal.
- If we can succeed in rebuilding a modicum of party government and party cohesion, there is little risk that we will veer from one extreme policy to its opposite, or that significant interest groups will become severely disaffected. We had party government for most of the time

before World War II, and putting the split over the constitutional entrenchment of slavery to one side, neither of these grievous consequences befell us. And in contrast to the United Kingdom, the constitutional role of the Supreme Court limits the extremes to which party government and party cohesion can take us. . . . [T]he Court will not permit party government to legislate beyond its constitutional rights. In part because of our diversity and size, but primarily because of the constitutional barriers, party government in America has never been efficient enough to achieve extreme and divisive results.

• Party government does not assure creative and effective government, but divided government comes close to assuring stagnant and ineffective government. All of the great presidents—Jefferson, Lincoln, Theodore Roosevelt, Wilson and Franklin Roosevelt—presided over party government. It is hard to think of a single major change of legislative policy in this century—with the exception of the Reagan 1981 tax cuts—that was adopted during a period of divided government, and that change occurred in the brief honeymoon period during the first year of President Reagan's term.

• A return to party government would not impair the congressional power to oversee executive performance and curb executive excesses. Nor would it restore the arbitrary power of party bosses and legislative leaders. Popular primaries and the democratization of congressional procedures are here to stay. These reforms, together with the penetrating surveillance of the investigative press, are sufficient guarantees that the basic constitutional checks and balances will continue to function. They do not depend on divided government to work. Teapot Dome, for example, was exposed during a time of party government, with Owen Roberts playing the same prosecutor's role that Archibald Cox was to fill in the Watergate scandal half a century later.[11]

Conclusion

Most Americans have little regard for political parties. In a 1980 survey, a majority thought that parties "do more to confuse the issues than to provide a clear choice on the issues," and most disagreed with the proposition that "it is better to be a firm party supporter than to be a political independent." Asked whether they agreed that "the best rule in voting is to pick a candidate regardless of party label," a large majority of respondents not only replied affirmatively, but did so on a seven-point scale to show great intensity of feeling.[12]

In light of these findings, we cannot expect people to trust parties to correct the ills of our electoral system, and so we find ourselves caught in a vicious circle. The weakness of the parties contributes to divided government. Divided government performs poorly, the poor performance leads to public cynicism, and that, in turn, further weakens the parties.

Repairing our battered electoral system will require that we break out of this pattern. The reforms outlined in Chapter 7 explore various ways of doing so.

3
Managing the Economy

Complaints about "the economy" are a perennial feature of politics. It would be difficult to name a period of American history when most people thought they were well off and safe from disturbing fluctuations.

In retrospect, perhaps, we can cite periods of relative stability and prosperity. The early 1960s seems to have been such a time. But there were dark spots even then. Michael Harrington called attention to "the other America," in a book that described grinding poverty in the midst of a generally affluent nation.[1] At about the same time, a book by Robert Heilbroner predicted a grim future. It was extremely urgent, he argued, for the government to invest billions of surplus dollars quickly to avoid a severe recession, but the political system resisted funding the obvious needs (such things as housing and other urban improvements), for reasons of ideology and for fear of social upheaval.[2] (Part of the solution, as it turned out, was to put a man on the moon, a program that consumed a huge amount of money without disrupting social arrangements at home.)

So Americans are quite right to take forecasts of economic doom with a grain of salt. But there are dangers on the other side, too: This callousness may cause us to ignore a truly serious challenge. The biblical writer Jeremiah warned against false prophets—people who cry "Peace, peace," when there is no peace.

The challenge of this chapter is to pinpoint the real dangers in the area of public finance and see how they are related to structural features of the American political system.

The Record of the 1980s

The 1980s has been a decade in which economic trends have been unusually hard to read. The task of the citizen is not easy when politicians of both parties and analysts of all persuasions have biases of their own.

Thus, one side points to a string of staggering budget deficits that caused the national debt to rise from just under $1 trillion in 1980 to over $2.3 trillion in 1988. The other side points out that deficits have been only 4.2 percent of GNP during that period, not too far above the average for the past 40 years.

The same discrepancies emerge when we turn to measures of performance for the economy as a whole. One side points out that— since November, 1982, when the "longest peacetime expansion in American history" began—the economy generated 15 million new jobs; interest rates, which had stood at more than 15 percent in 1980, fell to about 10 percent by 1988; and inflation went from a high of over 13 percent in 1980 to an annualized rate of about 4 percent in 1988.

The other side responds that the "jobless rate," which includes people the government no longer counts in the labor force, stood at 12.4 percent in March, 1988;[3] that the growth rate of American productivity was among the lowest of the developed countries;[4] and gross private domestic investment (by Americans, in American enterprise), which amounted to 17.5 percent of GNP between 1977 and 1980, fell to 15.9 percent between 1981 and 1987.[5] In light of the needs of a mature economy (not to mention the promise of a policy keyed to the supply side), it is also significant that savings as a share of the net national product fell from 6.4 percent in 1981 to 2.2 percent in 1987.[6]

These claims and counterclaims are difficult to sort out. Behind all the noise of political campaigns, though, it is possible to detect some real problems in economic management under our system of government: the build-up of public debt, low rates of savings and investment, the difficulty of relating the supply of money to the government's spending policies. These problems, which have become acute in recent years, were held in check for a century and a half principally by three factors:

1. the minimal impact of federal expenditures in the overall national economy;[7]
2. a cultural norm that prevailed until the 1930s, which required that government revenues and spending be kept at least roughly in balance, except perhaps in wartime, and that wartime debts ought to be paid as soon as possible;[8] and
3. a lack of accurate statistics, which meant that knowledge about the effects of public policies on the economy was impressionistic at best.

Since the middle of the twentieth century, however, the federal government has become a major participant in the nation's economy. In the mid-1980s, for example, it was directly responsible for nearly 25 percent of the gross national product. The question of whether the government spends more money than it takes in is no longer simply an ideological question. Surpluses and deficits have a major, measurable impact on the performance of the economy, pumping in billions of dollars if the government spends more money than it raises in revenues, and taking large sums of money out of circulation if the government takes in more revenues than it spends.

How has the federal government used this tremendous leverage? The answer in recent years (at least since the middle 1970s) has been that it has used it in a manner that virtually all political leaders, of both parties, deplore. At a time when there ought to have been surpluses in the federal budget in order to reduce inflation and interest rates, we have instead been incurring huge deficits. And at a time when we were importing more goods than we were selling abroad, we "strengthened" the dollar—partly to encourage foreign investors to buy our treasury's bonds—and thereby worsened our balance of trade.

This performance raises two important questions. If everyone deplored what we were doing, why did we continue to do it? And if what we were doing was so awful, why didn't the roof fall in?

Why Do Deficits Continue?

The first of these questions leads onto a darkling plain of political controversy. During the Reagan administration, if asked, who was responsible for the deficits, the president told us one thing: in his weekly radio address on September 27, 1986, he said, "We don't have deficits because you're undertaxed, we have deficits because Congress overspends. It's time Congress cut the federal budget and left family budgets alone."[9] The congressional leadership in turn pointed the finger right back at the president: It blamed his refusal to make realistic cuts in defense spending, then waited in vain for him to propose tax increases.[10] The public, for its part, was convinced that the deficit was a serious problem, but was disinclined, or unable, to pin the blame on any single person or group.[11]

As these contradictory assessments suggest, under our system of government it is nearly impossible to give credit to or pin the blame on anyone, even for gross outcomes. Who is responsible for budget deficits: the president or Congress? Who got inflation under control and caused interest rates to come down: Congress, the president (if so, which one?), or the Federal Reserve Bank? Who is responsible for the continuing imbalance of foreign trade?

These are not idle questions. If voters are to cast their ballots intelligently, it is essential to have answers. That is part of the constitutional problem: *No one* is fully responsible for what happens, so voters cannot reasonably choose between economic strategies. Our system provides no place where the power to make coherent, broad decisions can be gathered and exercised and then held accountable for the results.

Why Didn't the Roof Fall In?

The answer to the second question is that the effects of a lack of fiscal discipline tend to be corrosive, rather than explosive. Senator Daniel Patrick Moynihan (Democrat, New York) compares it to cancer. It is life-threatening—but if we wait until it hurts before we begin therapy, it will probably be too late.

The signs of debilitating illness are certainly there. Perhaps the most alarming is the way we have covered our debts. The principal reason that interest rates have come down, even while the government was covering a long string of budget deficits, is that foreign sources of capital moved in to purchase our Treasury bonds. It was thus unnecessary for the government to crowd out other American investors—industries wanting to retool, farmers, buyers of new homes and autos—by driving interest rates up higher. American government bonds were attractive to foreign buyers because our political system was stable and the dollar was "strong" (that is, highly valued, relative to other currencies). So we avoided a credit-crunch at home.

We did incur other costs, however. As public debt soared, interest payments as a proportion of federal expenditures soared. At a rate of 10 percent, the $200 billion deficit incurred in 1985 will consume $20 billion in interest payments annually forever (unless and until budget surpluses begin to pare it down, and that is not foreseeable). Servicing the national debt of $2.3 trillion claims the first $230 billion in federal revenues annually. We will be paying for the choices made in the 1980s as long as we live.

The other consequence of these public debts is that we mortgage our future to our creditors. It is almost unthinkable that bondholders would treat the United States the way bankers treated New York City in 1977, or as their international colleagues treated Poland, Brazil, and Third World debtors in recent years. But unless we can control the growth of our national debt, our creditors will be in a position to force draconian choices (cutbacks in funding for schools? scaling back medicare? trimming research on a missile-based defense system?) in return for refinancing arrangements. It may be that there are people in America who would welcome such discipline, provided it did not gore their own ox, but it would surely compromise American sovereignty.

The Trade Imbalance

One reason for the willingness of foreign investors to buy American Treasury bonds, as we have noted, was the "strength" of the dollar. This temporary advantage carried a high price. Our exports became more and more expensive to foreign consumers, and imported goods (cars, cameras, copiers) became a great bargain for Americans. But the result was a flight of American purchasing power to foreign producers and a loss of manufacturing jobs for American workers. This led to a series of severely negative trade balances.

Pretty soon the government was under intense political pressure to prevent further deterioration of American industry. One way of responding to the pressure was to protect American industries from foreign competition. Despite the administration's free-trade rhetoric, James Baker, then secretary of the treasury, admitted that the Reagan administration had granted "more import relief . . . than any of his predecessors in more than half a century." Market-sharing plans with our trading-partners resulted in what *Business Week* magazine called "managed trade." Economists estimate that these arrangements cost American consumers an extra $66 billion per year.[12]

Another strategy was to devalue the dollar. To make imports less attractive and American goods a better buy abroad, the Treasury Department negotiated a downward adjustment of the dollar's value. That quickly drove up the price of foreign goods in the United States. Its effect on the balance of trade, however, was slower, because of the ingrained preferences of consumers and the difficulty of overcoming bad habits that had developed among owners, managers and workers in America's protected industries.

There were some immediate effects, however. Owing to currency fluctuations, SONY of Japan was able to purchase the record division of CBS for a price that was half of what it would have been a year earlier.[13] Another indication was that the highest ranking American bank stood 28th in a listing of banks around the world in terms of the value of their deposits.[14]

At stake, in the eyes of many knowledgeable observers, is America's independence. In 1981, American investments abroad showed a net surplus of $140 billion over foreign investment here. By 1984, the margin had shrunk to $4.4 billion; by 1985, there was a negative balance of over $100 billion; and by 1988, foreign investment in American assets exceeded American investment abroad by $531 billion.[15]

The specter that lurks here is the purchase by foreign investors of assets vital to our national security and cultural sovereignty. There is currently a mechanism to review proposed foreign acquisitions of defense-related industries; we may need to extend it to other sensitive areas. Canadians have been deeply concerned, over the years, about American ownership of their publishing and entertainment industries. What if SONY had purchased Time, Inc., or Morgan Bank, instead of CBS records?[16]

Conclusion

This chapter has sketched the troubles of the economy and traced them to the fragmentation of responsibility within the political system. Because authority over key aspects of the economy is exercised by powers that are separated, and because parties are no longer able to unite voters and officials behind a coherent approach, our system's response to challenge and opportunity is sluggish and inconsistent.

We pay a high price for this inefficiency. We owe it to ourselves to consider carefully whether a simpler, stronger governmental system might make a positive contribution to economic management, and, if so, whether it would be consistent with other values we hold dear.

4
Controlling the Conduct of Foreign Relations

In the early 1940s, the United States finally took its place, irreversibly, as a leader among the world's nations. By the end of that decade, we had put aside our traditional insistence on isolation from European conflicts and had committed ourselves to a set of mutual defense treaties with nations not only in Europe, but in Latin America and Asia. During the four decades that followed, this radically altered environment presented stark and unprecedented challenges to the American system of checks and balances.

The purpose of this chapter is to sketch these developments as background for a consideration of reforms aimed at enabling the American constitutional system, in these vastly changed circumstances, better to "provide for the common defense, promote the general welfare, and secure the blessings of liberty."

Watershed: The Entry into World War II

The story begins with the American entry into World War II. The United States did not commit its armed forces to the struggle against German and Japanese imperialism until our allies were perilously close to defeat. Many observers, looking back on that period, believe that our hesitation encouraged the Axis powers to believe that we might never enter the conflict and thus contributed to the war's causes. That belief, coupled with the notion that President Franklin Delano Roosevelt had a clearer and more urgent sense of the looming danger than did Congress, fortifies the view that presidents ought to be dominant in the conduct of our foreign relations and national security policies.

It is thus important at least briefly to review the steps that led a reluctant nation to abandon its traditional isolationism and assume leadership of the Western alliance.

The roots of the process go back at least to 1934, when Senator Gerald Nye (Republican, North Dakota) conducted hearings about the munitions industry and its role in leading the United States into World War I. Congress reacted to Nye's findings, inconclusive though they were, by enacting a series of neutrality acts barring the sale and shipment of arms to any belligerent power. In 1937, Roosevelt invoked the neutrality statutes to keep the country out of the Spanish Civil War, but in October of that year he delivered a speech in Chicago in which he declared that the only way to preserve peace was to "quarantine" aggressors. Public opinion, sensitively reflected in Congress, bridled even at this tentative reformulation of the prevailing isolationism.

Three months later, Representative Louis Ludlow (Democrat, Indiana) proposed a constitutional amendment that would have required a national referendum before a congressional declaration of war could take effect. Ludlow's amendment was supported by 73 percent in a national poll. A strongly worded letter from Roosevelt helped to defeat it in the House, but its popularity with the general public showed that resistance to joining the alliance against Hitler was strong.

As war began to burn across Europe and the Far East, the United States began to take some tentative steps toward preparing its military forces for combat. Congress appropriated $1 billion for a "two-ocean navy," and in the 1940 presidential campaign, both major parties supported increased spending for national defense, aid to Britain, and strong defense of the western hemisphere. Yet both platforms still opposed participation in "foreign" wars.

In September 1940, Congress for the first time in its history passed a peacetime program of compulsory military service, by a fairly comfortable margin (232-124 in the House; 47-25 in the Senate). It was renewed a year later, four months before Pearl Harbor, this time by the margin of a single vote (203-202) in the House of Representatives. At the end of 1940, in a fireside chat, Roosevelt called for a production effort that would make the United States "the great arsenal of democracy." Thus, even at this late hour—over a year after the German invasion of Poland, six months after the fall of France, three months after Japan had entered into an alliance with Germany and Italy, and after Britain had lost nearly a thousand fighter planes in the Battle of Britain—the newly reelected president was building his policy on the premise that the United States might be able to stay out of the impending world war.

A year later (late 1941), Germany invaded Russia, Japan attacked Pearl Harbor, and Congress finally committed the United States to the alliance against Hitler. It was not until 1943, however, that American forces were able to reverse the tide of war in the Pacific, and not until

June, 1944, that the allies—under American command—were able to begin the counterattack across northern Europe.

U.S. involvement in World War II transformed the American outlook on the world—but not quickly or easily. Besides learning the necessity of military preparedness, Americans reluctantly concluded that the lack of responsible coordination between friendly governments was a contributing factor in the development of crises that led to World War II. World order needed a structure, backed by an organization with as much authority as nations were willing to grant it. Remembering our failure to join the League of Nations after World War I, we determined not to withhold our participation again.

At the same time, President Roosevelt knew that profound cultural changes would not happen overnight. Recalling the passion for a "return to normalcy" following World War I, he believed the American people would again be determined to return to peacetime pursuits as quickly as possible. And so he resisted long-term American commitments to the reconstruction of European affairs.

Adjustments After the War

Roosevelt was right about the post-war determination of Americans to return to peacetime occupations. Congress, ever sensitive to popular sentiments, insisted upon rapid and radical demobilization.

As it turned out, however, Roosevelt had been wrong about the resilience of American isolationism. He underestimated Stalin's determination to secure Soviet hegemony in eastern Europe and the Balkans, and he misgauged Americans' fear and fury at the advance of Soviet communism. He also did not anticipate the brilliance and persistence of those who shaped the American response, or the hard-won victory they would achieve over the voices of traditional American isolationism.

Post-war idealism found expression in the United Nations Charter. Post-war realism demanded a series of mutual-defense treaties and other arrangements that restated our hegemony over the western hemisphere (the Rio Pact) and bound us to Greece and Turkey, to our European allies (NATO), to Formosa, to several former European colonies in Southeast Asia, to the Philippines, and ultimately to our erstwhile enemy, Japan. The creation of this network of commitments was a bi-partisan effort, spanning the Truman-Acheson and Eisenhower-Dulles administrations. It promised that we would use our armed forces to defend over forty nations around the world from communist revolution and Soviet imperialism. We would defend their territory as if it were our own, and we would station our troops there as human evidence of our promise.

Korea

The first real test of this commitment came in Korea in June, 1950. On Saturday, June 24, communist troops from North Korea swarmed over the 38th parallel. The next day, the United Nations (UN) Security Council called for "an immediate cessation of hostilities" and asked members to assist the United Nations in gaining compliance with this resolution. (The resolution was adopted unanimously because the Soviet Union was boycotting the UN in protest against the exclusion of China.) On Tuesday, June 27, as the invasion continued, the Security Council formally called upon member states to help South Korea "repel armed attack." On the same day, President Truman ordered American air and sea forces to provide support for South Korean troops. Secretary of State Dean Acheson justified American involvement by noting that "all [allied] action in Korea has been under the aegis of the United Nations."

President Truman's actions, and especially Secretary Acheson's justification, alarmed many Americans, not least the leader of the Republican party in the Senate, Robert A. Taft, of Ohio. Immediately after the president announced his decision to intervene in Korea, Taft declared in the Senate that, if this incident passed without protest from the Congress, we would have "finally terminated . . . the right of Congress to declare war." By the turn of the year, it was clear that the conflict in Korea would not be a short-lived police action, and Taft's initial misgivings were hardening into a principled critique of the president's conduct. On January 5, 1951, he asserted in the Senate that the president had usurped authority in dispatching American forces to Korea without a congressional declaration. He argued that the UN Charter did not authorize the president to commit American forces to war, any more than the NATO pact authorized the president to send troops to Europe without congressional affirmation, as the Truman administration had clearly determined to do. Nor, said the minority leader, should appropriations passed by Congress be construed as an implicit declaration of support for presidential war-making. "We had no choice," he said, "but to back up wholeheartedly the boys who were fighting in Korea."[1]

Taft's denunciation of Truman alienated him from most of the foreign-policy establishment, but the concerns he voiced were shared by many thoughtful people. Senator Arthur Vandenberg (Republican, Michigan) had been one of the most severe critics of President Roosevelt's moves in support of the alliance against Hitler, but after the war he led the way to the new internationalism. In 1945, he was a leader of the American delegation that framed the UN Charter. (His principal contribution was the framing of Article 51, which provided for cooperation in international security.) Later, as chairman and ranking member of the Senate Foreign Relations Committee, he helped to forge the alliances that were designed to contain Soviet expansion.

At the time of Truman's decision to send troops to Korea, Vandenberg was home in Grand Rapids, dying of cancer. Commenting in letters to his Senate colleagues on the "great debate" going on in Washington, Vandenberg admitted he was troubled by the implications of President Truman's unilateral action. He noted the constitutional conflict, as old as the Constitution, between the president's responsibility as commander in chief and the responsibility of Congress to raise troops and declare war. It would be unwise and futile, he thought, for Congress to insist on explicit approval for each overseas troop deployment. He endorsed a distinction made by Governor Thomas E. Dewey of New York between the "commitment" and "deployment" of troops abroad, specifically stating that the latter was clearly the business of the commander-in-chief. At the same time, he thought the president had made a "great mistake" in not informing Congress immediately of his decision to send troops to Korea and requesting a resolution of support.[2] The lesson for the future, he thought, was that each branch ought to recognize the rightful role of the other in making war. "When there is time there ought to be consultation." If the emergency broke too quickly for consultation, Congress had no choice but to accept the president's responsibility as commander in chief to defend the country, but the president should "immediately notify Congress whenever an emergency requires the summary use of his personal responsibility."[3]

These ruminations of a dying senator in Michigan, whose personal odyssey from isolationism to engagement mirrored the nation's, foreshadowed a debate over the war powers that would last for the rest of the century.

Between Korea and Vietnam

In 1952, as the Korean War bogged down into a gory stalemate, Senator John Bricker (Republican, Ohio), who had been the Republican vice-presidential candidate in 1944, prepared a constitutional amendment to protect against the perceived dangers of presidential warmaking. In its original form, it sought to replace the supremacy clause of the Constitution (Article VI, second paragraph) with language that would have prevented the use of treaties or executive agreements to abridge rights reserved by the Constitution to individuals or state governments, or to authorize international organizations to abridge those rights.

The passions that swirled around Bricker's amendment were fueled by several court cases seeming to suggest that treaties and executive agreements might override state legislation.⁴ One that had particularly ominous import was the decision of a California appellate court in *Fujii vs. California,* voiding a state statute that prevented aliens from owning land on grounds that the statute was in conflict with the UN Charter.⁵ The California Supreme Court eventually overruled *Fujii,* and the United States Supreme Court later ruled that executive agreements were void if they conflicted with statutes or with the constitutional rights of citizens.⁶ These reassuring clarifications did not come soon enough, however, to prevent Bricker's amendment from garnering the support of 57 senators. Such support was not enough to amend the Constitution, particularly since many members of the House of Representatives did not share the Senate's concern over the abuse of the treaty power. It did serve, however, as a register of serious concern on the part of many members of both parties in Congress.

Even after the drive for Bricker's amendment weakened, the deeper problem remained: How could the government conduct foreign relations in the modern era without eroding constitutional and political safeguards? In the first decade after World War II, it was conservatives who felt this danger most keenly; liberals at that time tended to support the president. As Senator J. William Fulbright (Democrat, Arkansas) put it during the debate over Bricker's amendment, "It was never intended by the founding fathers that the president of the United States should be a ventriloquist's dummy sitting on the lap of the Congress."⁷

Later, however, after the bitterness over Vietnam, the roles were reversed. Liberals began to worry about presidential autocracy: again quoting Senator Fulbright, this time in 1971, "We have discovered that the president does not always know best, and that, indeed, the country would be far better off today if the Congress had been more assertive in the exercise of its constitutional role, which consists at least as much in assertion and criticism as it does in subservience."⁸ Meanwhile conservatives, particularly during the Nixon and Reagan years, became defenders of presidential prerogatives. Dick Cheney, for example, in a speech delivered just days before his appointment as secretary of defense in the Bush administration, pointed to what he called "patterns of congressional overreaching during the years of the Reagan administration." When Congress insists on a major role in the formulation of foreign policy, Cheney argued, "it takes traits that can be helpful to collective deliberation and turns them into a harmful blend of vacillation, credit-claiming, blame avoidance and indecision." The effect is not a *"transfer* of power from the president to the Congress, but a *denial* of power to the government as a whole."⁹

Constitutional Controversy Subsides

The decade between the demise of Bricker's amendment and the Gulf of Tonkin resolution was relatively quiet, from the standpoint of constitutional controversy. There was great public anxiety over the danger of nuclear annihilation, but there was also a broad consensus on the source of instability in the world (Soviet and Chinese communism) and about the responsibility of the United States to lead the defense of the "free world." In addition, the presidents of that period, Eisenhower and Kennedy, were committed to, and adept at, broad consultation in policy-making. Thus, Eisenhower blocked Dulles's attempt to take over the French role in Indochina when the European allies and leaders in Congress refused to give it their backing. And when Eisenhower was caught in misleading statements about the flight of a surveillance plane (the U-2) over the Soviet Union, he did not suffer much politically, because everyone understood the need for espionage. As for Kennedy, he took the world to the brink of nuclear war over the Soviet attempt to place missiles in Cuba, but at the time he was widely seen as acting with restraint, sometimes in the face of congressional urging that he be more aggressive in asserting American interests, and most observers were satisfied that he had consulted widely enough as the crisis unfolded.[10]

The Coming of the Imperial Presidency

The next two administrations, those headed by Lyndon Johnson and Richard Nixon, were plagued by constitutional controversy. Less than a year after assuming the presidency, Johnson used a brief skirmish of dubious origins in the Gulf of Tonkin as the pretext for a broadly worded resolution by Congress, authorizing him to take any action he deemed necessary to repel the threat to American interests in Southeast Asia. He asked for the resolution during a presidential campaign in which he presented himself as a leader of moderation, determined to avoid sending American boys to fight an Asian war. In that politically charged atmosphere, leaders in Congress did not hesitate to give him what he asked.

Before long, it became obvious that the president's policies in Indochina involved high costs. The price was apparently a surprise to the administration as well as to Congress, but it was Congress that had to vote the taxes and authorize the military build-up, including a military draft. Again (as with Korea), as the costs mounted Congress began to question not only the wisdom of the undertaking, but how it had begun.

The quagmire in Vietnam was a principal cause of the defeat of the Democratic ticket in the 1968 election. During the campaign, Nixon indicated that he had a "plan" to end the war in Vietnam. Soon after his inauguration, people began to look for evidence of the "plan" in operation. American casualties did gradually begin to diminish, infantry and marine units were called home, and the draft ended. Yet the war seemed to drag on; in fact, intensified bombing made it reverberate ever more loudly over television sets in American living rooms. Seeking a way to confine the war and bring it to an end, Congress repealed the Gulf of Tonkin resolution (without opposition from Nixon, who said that he was not relying on it, inasmuch as he was trying to bring the war to an honorable conclusion), and legislators began to look for ways to force the administration to replace military might with diplomatic negotiation.

The early 1970s was a time of great bitterness in relations between the president and Congress. The president wanted Congress to contribute to a united front in negotiations with the North Vietnamese. Meanwhile Congress was trying to force the president to bring the American involvement to an end.

The core of the issue was control over the use of armed forces. Ever since the Korean War, the executive had had a huge military force constantly at its disposal. In these circumstances, new in American history, the power that came from congressional control over the purse-strings was far less effective. As Senator Taft had realized as early as 1951, Congress could not abandon troops in the field. Gradually the realization dawned that Congress would have to gain access to the decision-making process at an earlier stage.

The War Powers Resolution

The year 1973 proved to be another watershed. The Watergate scandal broke, weakening the Nixon-Kissinger sway over foreign policy. With the political balances shifting, opponents of the Vietnam War in Congress were gradually able to force an American withdrawal. Meanwhile, leaders in Congress gained the passage, over President Nixon's veto, of the War Powers Resolution (WPR), a valiant but flawed attempt to correct the constitutional problems revealed by a quarter-century of standing armies and entangling alliances.

The concern of the sponsors, foremost among whom was Jacob Javits (Republican, New York), was that, since World War II, Congress had been excluded too often from decision-making about the use of American military force. Presented as a reaffirmation (not a modification) of the framers' intent, the resolution asserted that the president should, in every possible case, "consult with Congress" before committing American military forces to situations in which hostilities might erupt. At the same time, it was acknowledged that the president might sometimes have to send troops without such consultation. (Some commentators thought this clause granted a presidential role in initiating war even more clearly than the text of the Constitution itself.) In any case, the resolution required that the president report to Congress whenever he committed military forces to potentially dangerous situations. Unless Congress affirmed this commitment within sixty days, he was obliged to remove the forces; he could take an additional thirty days to accomplish the removal. Thus, in the absence of affirmative congressional action, the troops had to be out within ninety days.

It is not difficult to see the difficulties with this measure. What did "consult" mean? Did the president have to consult with Congress as a whole? If not, which part? What if the president did not report? Was it right to expect the courts to enforce this obligation on the president, when Congress had leverage of its own for an interbranch struggle, including the power of appropriations? Did the 60-day requirement make sense? Was it short enough to prevent our becoming inextricably committed to an unwise venture? Was it long enough to allow Congress to assess the wisdom of a particular engagement? Was it not an invitation to adversaries to hang on until the president was forced to remove American troops?

The WPR was thoroughly debated by Congress. Those who voted for it were experienced people, trying to make a system of separated powers work in modern foreign relations. They supported this resolution because it represented a spirit that was essential to the proper operation of the constitutional system: the spirit of mutual respect between Congress and the president. It provided a process that would serve well in circumstances where there was consensus and when everyone had time to proceed at an eighteenth-century pace.

As events would soon show, however, it did not work very well at the flash-points of modern world affairs.

Shortcomings of the War Powers Resolution

Consulting in an Emergency. The first problem with the WPR was that it was sometimes impossible to conduct meaningful consultations in an emergency. President Ford tried, despite his skepticism about the WPR in general,[11] to abide by its requirements of consultation and reporting. Even so, in responding to the Cambodian attack on the *Mayaguez* in 1975, he was simply unable to assemble the leaders of Congress in time. The recovery of the *Mayaguez* crew was in itself a brief, minor episode (though it did cost the lives of forty-five American marines), but it foreshadowed the terrible responsibility that a president would have in the event of a sneak nuclear attack.

The responsibility to repel sudden attacks has to lie somewhere; the framers believed that it must lie with the president. Any workable rules for interbranch consultation had to allow for such emergencies.

But if the exception for emergencies is unavoidable, it is also dangerous. It can be used to cover a multitude of situations. Was it an emergency precluding consultation when President Reagan sent American forces to invade Grenada, or when he dispatched bombers to Libya? In both cases, the president's initiative went essentially unchallenged because the operations were over before Congress could fully engage the question of procedures. But the actions set precedents; many observers thought they revealed a serious weakness in the WPR.

Covert Actions. The second problem has to do with covert actions. If one can conceive in principle of agreements, troop deployments, and even military actions that ought not to be debated in public, and yet one continues to believe that no one person ought to be constitutionally able to commit American men and materiel to hostilities, then the procedures in the WPR were inadequate. There needed to be a mechanism for secret consultation between the executive and legislative branches.

This was no easy matter. In theory, it can be argued that the powers of Congress (including the power to declare war, from which these other decisions derive) cannot be delegated, not even to a part of itself. Even if you concede that point, however, and grant that certain congressional leaders may act for the whole body, there are other problems: Can members of Congress, even those who hold leadership positions, be trusted with national security secrets? And is there not a danger of cooptation? Might not the president disarm the criticism of congressional leaders by informing them of activities with which they would like publicly to disagree?

Again, these objections to the WPR are pretty obvious. Yet Congress felt compelled to do something about a situation that had gotten out of hand. Only in 1969, for example, did the Senate learn of security arrangements that President Johnson had made with Thailand four years earlier. Only in 1973 did it come out that President Nixon had misled when he said that the invasion of Cambodia that began in April, 1970, was the first time that American and South Vietnamese troops had attacked the sanctuaries in Cambodia. In light of these revelations, it seemed imperative for Congress to establish that secret military operations could no longer be undertaken on the president's authority alone.

Accordingly, in 1974, Congress passed the Hughes-Ryan amendment to the Foreign Assistance Act. It required that the president inform Congress in a "timely manner" of any covert intervention abroad. In practice, this meant informing the committees on foreign relations and foreign affairs, appropriations, armed services and intelligence. Thus, 200 members of Congress, not to mention many staff members, were entitled by law to know about all secret military operations abroad— a plainly unworkable standard.

In 1980, Congress replaced the Hughes-Ryan formula with the Intelligence Oversight Act, which limited the reporting to the intelligence committees of the two houses and assigned the responsibility for reporting to the Director of the CIA and other department heads involved in covert activities, rather than to the president himself. The requirement of presidential approval for all such actions was retained, however, and the president was given authority to make exceptions in the event of emergencies.

The Iran-contra scandal of 1986–87 proved that these statutory controls on covert actions were not foolproof. The Reagan administration failed to send to the intelligence committees a timely, written record of the president's "finding" that the sale of arms to Iran was necessary; in fact, he never informed the intelligence committees about crucial details of the operation at all.

For these lapses he performed acts of contrition, such as acknowledging in a letter to Senators David Boren (Democrat, Oklahoma) and William Cohen (Republican, Maine), co-chairs of the Senate Intelligence Committee, that the government "worked better" when the president cooperated closely with Congress. The president promised to keep congressional leaders informed about future covert operations.

But Reagan's agreement could not bind future administrations, and Congress seemed not to know how to improve the system to prevent future abuses. It had been only a dozen years since the "long, national nightmare" of Watergate was supposed to have taught an unforgettable lesson about the dangers of presidential abuse of war powers, yet the monitory effect seemed already to have been lost. No remedial legislation on controlling covert action passed through Congress during the waning days of the Reagan administration.

Warfare by Proxy. Another situation not covered by the WPR was second-hand warfare, a leading example of which was the support extended to the "contra" rebels in Nicaragua by the Reagan administration. Here was an application of military force in which the United

States had a vital part, even though American troops were not directly involved. Congress could have controlled it, one would have thought, by the power of appropriation: To give material aid to the contras, Congress had to vote the funds.

Or did it?

In 1982 and 1983, the administration, with the approval of the intelligence committees of both houses, applied nearly $40 million of covert aid, through the CIA, to the contras. (In 1983, there was a stipulation that none of this assistance could be used to train or equip contras for the overthrow of the Sandinistas nor to provoke a military exchange between Nicaragua and its neighbors.) In 1984, for the first time, Congress appropriated funds for military assistance to the contras.

In March and April, 1984, it came to light that the CIA had participated in mining Nicaraguan harbors, without notifying the intelligence committees. Congress responded to the public outcry by cutting off all aid to the contras through an amendment to the omnibus appropriations act which read:

> No funds available to the Central Intelligence Agency, the Department of Defense or any other agency or entity of the United States involved in intelligence activities may be obligated or expended for the purpose or which would have the effect of supporting, directly or indirectly, military or paramilitary operations in Nicaragua by any nation, group, organization, movement or individual.[12]

By this amendment, named for its principal sponsor, Representative Edward Boland (Democrat, Massachusetts), Congress discontinued all legal assistance to the contras for almost two years, beginning in mid-1984.[13] The administration, still determined to overthrow the Sandinistas, turned to other alternatives: the solicitation of gifts from private sources or from third countries, plus the illegal transfer of public funds. Thus money made its way to the contras from donors who were accorded "photo opportunities" with the president and whose gifts were solicited by members of the White House staff; from foreign nations that rely on protection and favorable trading arrangements with the United States; and from the diversion of profits earned from the sale of arms to Iran.[14]

The most upsetting aspect of the revelations about fund-raising for the contras was the president's remark that he found nothing wrong with it. He was referring specifically to the solicitation of funds from private individuals in this country. So long as public funds were not used, he asked, what was wrong with that? The answer, of course, was that it cut the purse strings which the Constitution put in the hands of Congress for controlling executive acts. The president simply refused to accept the verdict of Congress on his policy. The sale of arms to Iran went on for over a year, and support to the contras contrary to the Boland amendment for nearly two years, before disclosure forced their termination.

The inescapable conclusion is that the rule of law was unable to restrain a president who took the position that his constitutional powers made the laws inapplicable to him or to White House aides acting in his name.

Long-Term, Low-Intensity Conflicts. Congress in 1973 designed the WPR to prevent another Vietnam. Experience with the most dangerous war of the 1980s—the naval combat in the Persian Gulf—suggests that it does not work very well in situations that require sustained military pressure.

Why not? If a consensus agreed that the American navy should patrol the Persian Gulf and protect neutral, commercial shipping, why could the president not report that this was what he intended to do, and Congress resolve, after a sixty-day period of watching the results, to affirm it, or, if it didn't like the results, to end it?

The answer is that a government cannot conduct foreign relations by resolution. The WPR obliges the president to report to Congress when he introduces armed forces into a potentially hostile situation (the Persian Gulf certainly qualifies), but it does not oblige him to say why, in detail, or how he plans to proceed. In most instances, and certainly in this one, that is only right, since it is impossible to say in advance exactly what may be required. On the other hand, a statement in generalities from the president would be of little value to Congress in limiting the engagement. So the president, if he reported at all (he did not, in this case), would do so in very broad terms. Congress in its resolution sixty days later could not be much more specific, without undermining the effort.

On the other hand, Congress would not want to give the president carte blanche. It might be better, from the standpoint of congressional control over the engagement, to have no resolution at all until legislators were clear how they wanted to limit it. (That is presumably why Congress decided not to trigger the 60-day period by resolving that armed forces had entered a hostile situation.)

Conclusion

The WPR was a laudable attempt to induce cooperation between the branches and establish a timetable that drives officials to collaborate. Yet it has not solved the problem of compelling reluctant officials to cooperate, and it has left many well-intentioned people frustrated and angry at their inability either to abide by it or to propose improvements. It has been resisted by presidents as an infringement on their constitutional responsibility to conduct foreign relations and deploy troops in the national defense. Courts have been reluctant to enforce it, because that would involve second-guessing judgments which the Constitution commits to the political branches. And Congress has not been able to insist on strict compliance because it recognizes that its terms are inappropriate in some cases.

The WPR represented an attempt by experienced legislators to adapt the Constitution to the conditions of late 20th century warfare. It has not worked. It provides a continual reminder of the desirability of cooperation between the branches, and that is worth something. But as a process for achieving that cooperation and as a standard for measuring it, it has failed.

PART TWO

DO WE NEED STRUCTURAL REFORM?
Pro and Con

5
Keeping Pace with the Times:[1] The Case for Structural Reform

Two hundred years ago, America's political leaders decided that the existing national government was inadequate. Commerce among the thirteen states was stalled, it was impossible to pay the public debt, and foreign governments showed no respect for the young nation's diplomats. Sensing that their dream of independent nationhood was slipping away from them, they called delegates to a convention in Philadelphia to consider whether reforms were possible.

Some of the delegates to the Federal Convention of 1787 urged caution, fearing that the citizens of the new republic would not support radical reforms. But bolder counsel prevailed. The Convention drew up a new constitution, providing greater power for the national legislature, a separately elected president, an independent judiciary, and more responsibility for the federal government in relation to the states.

Within a year, the American people made up their minds to inaugurate the newly modelled government. Almost everyone had misgivings. Some thought that the Senate was too aristocratic; others feared the centralization of power at the federal level; many hated to inaugurate the new government before a bill of rights was securely in place. But most were ready to take a chance, because they believed that the structure was basically sound. Besides, changes could be made later, as they were needed.

The founders were quite candid about the need for future reappraisal. Concluding his argument for ratification in the last *Federalist* paper, Alexander Hamilton drew on the authority of the Scottish philosopher, David Hume. In an essay on "The Rise and Progress of the Arts and Sciences," Hume had written, "To balance a large state . . . on general laws is a work of so great difficulty that no human genius, however comprehensive, is able, by the mere dint of reason and reflection, to effect it. The judgment of many must unite in the work; experience must guide their labor; time must bring it to perfection, and the feeling of inconveniences must correct the mistakes which they *inevitably* fall into in their first trials and experiments." There would be opportunity later, Hamilton wrote, to adjust the framework as experience revealed the need.[2]

We mock this spirit of practical wisdom if we refuse to reexamine the Constitution, even its separation of powers, as familiar and settled as that aspect may seem.

Modern Democracy and Constitutional Reform

Those who warn against a modern reassessment of constitutional verities sometimes question whether we can recreate the conditions that made it possible to frame a Constitution in the eighteenth century. The original framers worked for more than three months in secret, did not reveal their handiwork until it was complete, and did not publish a record of their deliberations until all the framers were dead.

Obviously such secrecy would be impossible today. Newspaper and television reporters would swarm all over any conclave that had authority to consider amendments, particularly if it began to appear that changes might actually be in the offing. Interest groups would examine the proposals to see what effect they might have; and if they felt any threat or opportunity, they would mobilize their followings with all the arts of modern mass communications. Ultimately, no substantial changes could be made unless overwhelming majorities of citizens became convinced they were needed. Let us not mince words: A move to reshape our constitutional system in any fundamental way would touch off political convulsions. Indeed, such a move is probably unlikely unless the body politic is already experiencing turmoil.

But the fear of this process is finally an act of despair against democracy. Since mid-century, we have experienced some tremendous mobilizations of popular sentiment: overthrowing racial segregation, ending the Vietnam War, demanding the removal of a president before the next election. These were tumultuous affairs, and they were not resolved by the ordinary processes of politics. They strained our civic fabric. But as the public mind became convinced that changes had to be made, ways were found to accomplish them without permanent damage. On the contrary, the necessary surgery produced lasting benefits.

Structural Change Is Not New

Our political history already contains many examples of structural changes in our political system, some achieved by constitutional amendment, others not. By constitutional amendment, we have ended slavery and greatly expanded the electorate. We have uprooted senators from their state legislatures and replanted them in statewide electorates. We have shortened by two and a half months the period between a presidential election and inauguration.

Perhaps even more striking are the basic structural changes we have adopted without amending the Constitution at all. The invention of the political party with its quadrennial nominating convention is one example. More recently, the move to a system of nomination by primary elections revolutionized the process for choosing presidents. Nothing is more crucial to a political system than the process for choosing the head of state. By substituting primaries for conventions as the normal mode of nomination, we became the first nation in human history to nominate its candidates for chief of state by direct popular election. We did it almost inadvertently.

Another fundamental change adopted without constitutional amendment is the so-called independent regulatory commission (such as the Federal Trade Commission, the Securities and Exchange Commission, and the Federal Reserve Board). The agencies—the Supreme Court has called them "quasi-legislative, quasi-executive and quasi-judicial"—transcend the separation of powers by combining rule-making, enforcement and the settlement of disputes in a single governmental body. Congress first created them around the turn of the century, when the American economy became too complex for regulation by statute.

So we have already made many structural changes. We will certainly have to make more if our system is to adapt and meet the challenges of the third American century. It stands to reason that a framework designed over two centuries ago may need adjustment. Changes in the political environment since then—changes in our social fabric, in the demands on the government for the regulation of a complex modern economy, and in the integration of our affairs into a global framework—alone indicate a need for reconsideration.

Problems in the Existing System

In addition to these somewhat philosophical reasons for thinking about fundamental political reform, there are pressing practical considerations. One cannot read a daily newspaper or watch the news on television without realizing that the American system is operating under immense strain as we approach the beginning of the twenty-first century.

The most serious problems lie in the electoral system. Nothing is more important for a nation committed to democracy than its elections.

Many specific problems in this area are analyzed elsewhere in this book: the excessive length and cost of campaigns, the poor quality of the exchanges between candidates, the fixed calendar. Our low rates of turnout on election day, relative to those of other constitutional democracies, are downright ominous. Some analysts try to comfort us by suggesting that low turnout rates may reflect passive satisfaction, that high turnout rates (as in Germany in the early 1930s) often reveal fevers in the body politic, but we all know that when only half of the eligible electorate bothers to vote even for president (and for other offices, even lower than that), we have a problem.

Another area of great concern during the past decade has been the mounting national debt, augmented each year by huge new budget deficits. There is plenty of blame to go around for this worsening situation. Public officials have shirked their responsibility, and public opinion has been all too eager to ignore the situation or accept easy reassurances.

We need to recognize that there may be a structural problem. Lloyd Cutler has called attention to the fact that deficits as a percentage of the gross national product have exceeded 3 percent only seven times since the end of World War II. In each of these cases, control over the White House and Congress was divided between the two major parties. Never, during this period, has the deficit been as high as 3 percent when both branches were held by the same party. This may be a coincidence—but it seems wise to consider the possibility that it reflects a fundamental structural defect in our political system.

The management of foreign policy is yet another great cause for concern. Whether one believes that Congress meddles unduly in this area or that presidents have been abusing their powers, it is clear that the intended collaboration between the branches has broken down frequently in recent years. Presidents and their staffs, frustrated by congressionally imposed restrictions and fearing leaks, have launched important diplomatic, military and covert activities in secret and without consulting Congress. Recurring episodes of this kind have produced a series of spectacular investigations and have badly damaged our credibility abroad, but they have not as yet led Congress to enact any promising reforms of the process.

On the other side, Congress has sometimes been accused of attempting to "micro-manage" foreign policy, interfering unwisely in the work of the executive branch. Again, structural difficulties may lie at the root of these fruitless conflicts. Congress, regularly dominated by people not of the president's party, feels shunted aside, particularly at times of national crisis. Frustrated and determined to make its presence felt, it throws sand in the wheels of the administration's policy.

Another way of viewing this problem in foreign relations is to consider how it looks from a foreign perspective. Foreign governments, whether friendly or not, get mixed signals from the American side, and they are inclined either to doubt our firmness and reliability as allies or to test our resolve. Either way, we run unnecessary hazards, not so much because of honest differences over policy, but because of unpredictable and unproductive forays by one branch or the other into areas where they ought not to venture alone.

Parties: The Vital Center

The root of the structural problem lies in the weakness of the parties: their failure to induce candidates to stand behind a coherent platform or program, however generally phrased; their inability to join their successful candidates, once elected, behind a drive to carry out the party's program; and their refusal to present themselves collectively for an electoral verdict at the next election.

Historically, parties in America have been more strongly committed to patronage than ideology. Still, until fairly recently, they did tend to present candidates as a team of elected officials who stood or fell together, to a far greater extent than is the case today.

As Lloyd Cutler has pointed out, "party government" (defined as the control of the White House and of both houses of Congress by the same party) prevailed more than three-quarters of the time between 1796 and 1945, but less than half of the time since 1945, and less than one-third of the time since 1968.[3] Since World War II, divided government has become not the exception, but the rule.

It comes from a weakening of party loyalty. Fewer people today vote a straight ticket. From 1900 to 1908, only 4 percent of the nation's congressional districts gave a majority to one party's candidate for president, but elected the other party's congressional candidate. In 1984, almost half of the nation's congressional districts gave President Reagan a majority while electing a Democratic member of the House.

The problem stems partly from the tendency to reelect incumbents. Three recent presidents (Eisenhower, Nixon and Reagan) were reelected by margins as large as 16 to 23 percent, while voters were returning Democratic majorities to the House all three times, and to the Senate twice.[4] Since mid-century, over 90 percent of Senate and House incumbents who run for reelection have been successful. In 1984, the success rate was 96 percent, and in 1988, a remarkable 98 percent. Cutler draws a telling contrast to the pattern in Canada: ". . . when the Canadian Liberal Party fell from power in the 1984 election, the percentage of incumbents who ran and won reelection was a mere 61 percent, and for Liberal Party incumbents, it was only 26 percent."[5]

The problem is well illustrated by the results of recent national elections. Since World War II, control of the White House has shifted from one party to the other five times: in 1952, 1960, 1968, 1976, and 1980. Only once (in 1952) did partisan control over the House follow the presidential lead; and in the Senate, only twice (1952 and 1980). Otherwise, members of Congress campaigning for reelection were able to resist the trend in the other branch. The following table shows the results in Congress in these years of partisan shifts in the White House[6]:

Year	Senators and Representatives Reelected Despite Their Party's Loss of White House
1952 (D)	187 out of 208
1960 (R)	142 out of 145
1968 (D)	246 out of 257
1976 (R)	125 out of 134
1980 (D)	231 out of 268

The presidential campaign responds to a different drummer from the one heard in congressional campaigns. When majorities in Congress are isolated to this extent from political trends reflected elsewhere in the system, the voters cannot deliver a mandate on national policy. Claims that one or the other represents the true will of the people are readily dismissed as self-serving rhetoric. The point is, the parties have not been able, since mid-century, to organize a coherent expression of the popular will.

The essence of democracy is politics, and politics without parties in a large, diverse nation is incoherent and unaccountable to the people. Without strong parties, the field is abandoned to other organized groups. The advantage lies with those who have the financial means and skills to put together an organization and send representatives to Washington. Those abilities are fairly widely distributed in modern America, but they are not universal. Parties are by far the broadest representative of political sentiment. That is one reason they are so hard to discipline. But it also makes them potentially the best vehicle for achieving "government of the people, by the people, for the people."

Woodrow Wilson once remarked that, in a system of separated powers, he was unable to advance a cause he believed in by voting for any individual—no, he said, "not even if I vote for myself." He meant that an individual in office, even a president, depends on the cooperation of others to achieve his goals. A strong party can help a president to secure that cooperation—and, because such a relationship is reciprocal, a strong party can hold the president accountable to his fellow-partisans. V. O. Key had this in mind when he described party as the web that holds the government together.

If parties are weak, that coherence is lacking, and the government cannot act to meet challenges. Then two tendencies come to the fore: either the government lapses into confusion, stalemate and paralysis, or people in high office, frustrated and anxious, begin to act on their own. When the latter happens, the people tend to respond, initially at least, with relief and gratitude, but in due course, abuses come to light, investigations begin, and the government collapses into recrimination.

It is always tempting to believe that our problems stem from the failures of individual office-holders, or from the daunting character of modern problems. In fact, there is good reason to believe that our public officials are at least as capable as their American predecessors or foreign counterparts. As for the difficulty of modern problems, that too is exaggerated. We have great expertise at our disposal, and we have no difficulty framing proposals. What we lack is the capacity to organize a political will behind any promising approach, and that is a structural problem.

A Call for Untrammeled Thinking

In his commencement address at Tufts University in 1982, C. Douglas Dillon tells of an interview given by the British ambassador in Washington, Sir Nicholas Henderson. Asked for his views of our government, the ambassador said, "You don't have a system of government. You have a maze of government. In [other countries] if you want to persuade the government . . . or find out their point of view on something, it's quite clear where the power resides. It resides with the government. Here [in America] there's a whole maze of different corridors of power. There's the administration. There's the Congress. There are the staffers. There's the press. . . ." The ambassador concluded by observing that this situation "makes life in Washington . . . very much more exciting, difficult and varied than anywhere else." Dillon suggests that the ambassador would have been more frank if he had said, "That's what makes the life of a foreign diplomat in Washington so difficult, frustrating and dangerous."[7]

Dillon goes on to draw a lesson from these comments. "There is no way in which Congress can formulate or implement foreign policy, and there is no way for the president to have assurance that the Congress will support the executive branch in carrying out the policies formulated by it." This situation, he says, was viable for the first century and a half of our national life, when we lived in relative isolation. It continued to work in the immediate post-war era, when our military and financial power dominated the world. But in today's complex and turbulent world, ambiguity and indecision carry a high cost.

Concerned about these developments, many scholars have been led to consider various modest reforms, such as changes in the terms of members of Congress or public financing of campaigns. But these, argues Dillon, do not address the "much more serious problem" of the inability to place responsibility for the conduct of government on a person or group that can be held accountable for its stewardship. This situation can only be remedied by a truly significant shift to some form of parliamentary system, one that would "eliminate or sharply reduce the present division of authority in Washington." He notes that such a shift is "unlikely to come about except as a result of a crisis that is very grave indeed, one that I hope we never have to face." But we ought, he says, to be considering it, because such a crisis, if it comes, may come quickly, and we dare not face it unprepared.[8]

Continuing the American Quest

As our economy develops and takes its place in a shifting global context, as our population grows and becomes more diverse, as our evolving moral sensitivities present new challenges, as new technologies require more sophisticated controls, new demands confront our system of governance. And because we are committed to self-government, these complicated problems challenge not just our elites, but the people of this nation.

That is why these modern developments have implications for the way we govern ourselves. Because our Constitution has worked so well for over two centuries, we have grown unused to thinking about the structure of governance. Citizens of the founding generation, from the town cobbler to James Madison, were quite at home in a discussion of whether a legislature should have one chamber or two, how the branches should check one another, and whether the type of economy we had, and were about to have, would be better served by a stronger national government.[9] We have lost that knack. Some of our political scientists have told us that structures of government do not matter very much. As for the average citizen, he or she has grown complacent about the durability of the Constitution. We live in turbulent times. People are very eager to believe that the Constitution, at least, is a sheet-anchor.

This complacency is no longer tenable. The evidence is accumulating that our political system is under great strain. The links are weakening between the people and government, and between officials who serve in different branches. What is at risk is democracy, the promise that people are capable of governing themselves.

Theorists have long known that democracies tend to be sluggish. Jefferson wrote in the Declaration of Independence that "all experience hath shown that mankind are more disposed to suffer while evils are sufferable, than to right themselves by abolishing forms to which they are accustomed." But American experience has also shown that we are capable of rousing ourselves to a moral imperative. In 1861, Abraham Lincoln urged us to "disenthrall ourselves." "The dogmas of the quiet past are inadequate to the stormy present," he said. "As our case is new, so must we think anew, and act anew." A reluctant nation responded to that call and made terrible sacrifices to correct a deep fault in our political system.

No one thinks that a comparable effort will be needed today. But we do need to "disenthrall ourselves." We need to face our difficulties and trace them to their roots—and if the tracing reveals faults in our basic institutions and in the processes that link them together, we must be prepared to make changes.

6
Don't Fix It: The Case Against Structural Reform

The case against fundamental reform of the American political system begins with an instinct, both widely and deeply felt in the American political culture. The Constitution establishes a political system that has worked remarkably well through two turbulent centuries.

Americans are a lively, sometimes boisterous people. We come from varied backgrounds; we live in different regions; we earn our bread in different ways. We disagree about almost everything. But we all love the Constitution. We deeply believe that it protects our rights and gives us all a fair chance to compete for political goals.

It is a mistake to take this shared confidence in the Constitution for granted. During the past two hundred years, other Western nations (France, Germany, Italy) have been badly distracted and torn asunder by struggles over constitutional questions. The newer nations of the western hemisphere—many of them, like us, former colonies of European nations—have also had great difficulty finding broadly acceptable constitutional formulas. We ought not to assume that the consensus that has enabled us to avoid these troubles is permanent or indestructible.

Our own political history has been anything but tranquil. It has included a ghastly civil war over slavery and the nature of the federal union, as well as struggles over the rights of racial minorities and of women.[1] But through it all, we have joined in affirming the notion of individual rights and the basic political process established at the end of the eighteenth century.[2] That consensus seems nothing short of miraculous, in the context of human political history. The founders must have discovered something profoundly correct. Obviously their system needs to be adjusted as the nation develops and matures and as it becomes integrated into the world of nations. But we would be fools indeed, in light of this record of success, to tamper with the basic design.

What *did* they discover? What are the features of the basic design which has worked so well and with which it would be foolish to tamper in any fundamental way?

First, of course, is the separation of powers: assigning the two basic political functions—law-making and administration—to distinct authorities and keeping them both independent and strong by rooting them in distinct electoral processes. It was brilliant also to make their functions overlap, to give each a hand in the other's activities, so that they might check one another. Thus the president can veto legislation that threatens his constitutional prerogatives or leadership, but the Senate can block his appointments if they seem corrupt, and Congress can deny funds for ventures that lack public support. In these ways the system forces elected leaders to cooperate and gives them means and incentive to block action if necessary.

Above all, the framers found a way to balance the two basic requirements of government: the need on the one hand for strong leadership and the capability to take vigorous action in emergencies; the need on the other hand to keep this awesome power accountable. That is the great puzzle in building a constitutional framework, and it is the great achievement of the framers to have discovered how to solve it, at least in the American context.[3]

An old aphorism holds that a merciful God protects children, drunkards, and the United States of America. Admirers of the Constitution have a more secular explanation for our survival. In the presidency we have an institution that is able to take command in times of grave national danger, one that can take decisive action by focussing and concentrating the powers that are normally separated. Thus Lincoln in 1861; thus FDR in 1933 and again in 1941.

Clinton Rossiter, not unsympathetically, called this capacity to suspend the separation of powers in an emergency "constitutional dictatorship." All constitutional systems, Rossiter argued, have to be able to mobilize their energies to meet situations that threaten their survival. The concentration of executive powers in the president gives the United States this capacity to deal with emergencies.

Rossiter went on to warn that there needed to be firm safeguards, lest a nation begin to resort routinely to the facilities of "dictatorship." The absence of such regulations, he wrote, had contributed to the demise of the Weimar Republic in Germany between the World Wars. He urged Americans to enact rules for invoking and terminating the president's emergency powers.[4] Others, taking a different tack, hold that we are already protected from the abuse of the president's powers.

The system works like a pendulum. When we confront grave danger and the nation moves to meet it, power flows to the president. After the danger has passed, Congress, reflecting the public desire to return to normal pursuits, dismantles the machinery of emergency and resumes its accustomed place, especially by asserting its power over the purse-strings. And if the public concludes that the president is abusing his authority, Congress has the means to reign him in. Thus: Watergate, in which President Nixon was forced to resign as Congress moved to impeach him. As President Ford said, articulating the national sigh of relief, "The long national nightmare is over. Our Constitution works."

Response to Specific Complaints

The Deficits. To arguments that the budget and trade deficits demonstrate the need for basic structural reform, defenders of the Constitution reply that they show no such thing. First, they insist that recent American budgetary deficits are not all that unusual. James Q. Wilson presents a table, based on data from the Organization for Economic Cooperation and Development, that shows the United States ranking 10th in a list of 14 industrial democracies in terms of the budget deficit for 1984, measured as a percentage of a nation's gross national product.[5] Professor Wilson notes that all of the other nations on his list—all of those with higher deficits and the few whose deficits are smaller than the United States—have parliamentary systems.

If budget deficits are a problem at all, say these defenders of the American system, they are a political problem. The deficits of the 1980s arose (depending on one's political point of view) because Congress refused to make the necessary cuts; or because President Reagan gave no leadership on the issue, but instead presented a series of budgets that were not balanced; or because President Reagan and Congress conspired to perpetuate the deadlock. In any case, the remedy is not to revise the Constitution, but to elect people whose economic policies are sound.

The truth is that the American people are not convinced that deficits are a serious problem. If they were, they would support candidates who take the problem seriously, who prescribe the bitter medicine (cuts and taxes) necessary to solve it. And if the problem *is* serious despite the "conspiracy" between candidates and voters to ignore it, then we may have to suffer some before we address it. That, however, is a problem of the education of public opinion, and it would not be solved in a way consistent with democratic constitutionalism by strengthening the president's hand.

It takes a democracy longer to understand problems. Authoritarian regimes, whether benevolent or otherwise, tend to be quicker. The

American system, with its abundant provisions for delay and deflection, is particularly prone to trouble on this score. But it is not incapable of action, once its mind is made up. As Lord Bryce noted over a century ago, "It is not for Congress to go faster than the people. When the country knows and speaks its mind, Congress will not fail to act."[6] It is still true.

The Stern Challenges of Modernity. It is sometimes contended that our eighteenth-century Constitution may have been well suited to the nineteenth and early twentieth centuries, when an energetic people were settling the continent and when the ocean kept us isolated from Europe's conflicts. Then perhaps we needed only a light hand to maintain public order and defend our frontier settlements. Our situation now is different. We need positive regulation of a tightly integrated national economy, and we need firm yet accountable direction of our involvement in a global economy. A constitution of separated powers, it is said, cannot give us these things.

But, reply the defenders, our political system has proven to be greatly adaptable. It retains the virtues of old: responsive legislation, vigorous administration, checks and balances, independent courts, strong defense of basic rights. And it adapts to new challenges.

Was Congress unable to regulate modern industries by legislation? The system created the so-called independent regulatory commission to make and enforce rules for such modern enterprises as railroads, the securities business, electronic communications, and the banking system.

Did we need to escape from interest-group pressures for protectionism? Congress helped to establish mechanisms for delegating a measure of control over foreign commerce to administrative agencies, which were presumably less vulnerable to such pressures.

Did we need to reapportion legislative districts? The Supreme Court eventually stepped into the breach.

We find a way. And we will find a way to meet current challenges. Sometimes the Supreme Court blocks a particular adaptation, declaring it "unconstitutional." The Court struck down the legislative veto, finding that it gave Congress too much power to second-guess the decisions of administrators. It gutted the enforcement mechanism of the deficit-reduction plan developed by Senators Gramm, Rudman and Hollings, on grounds that it diluted the president's responsibility for the execution of the laws. Congress and the president must find other ways to attain the desired results. They will. They always have. Congress will learn to legislate more carefully (forestalling the need for the legislative veto), and it will act responsibly on fiscal matters, rather than trust an automatic mechanism to do the dirty work.

War Powers. One truly new problem, it is often contended, involves the use of war powers. Never before the middle of the twentieth century did American presidents claim inherent power to take this nation to war. Now we are routinely led to war by presidents, acting on their own authority. The War Powers Resolution has failed to force presidents to bring Congress into the process. Does this not suggest the need for new constitutional restraints?

No, say the defenders, it does not. Careful research has shown that presidents have repeatedly, throughout American history, applied military force against the nation's enemies without declarations of war or any other explicit legislative authorization.[7] It has been clear from the beginning that the Constitution intends for the president to conduct the nation's foreign relations. This responsibility necessarily includes the power to deploy military force; that is why the Constitution makes the president commander in chief. It is all part of the same job.

Congress retains the power to declare war, and it has the power to raise and equip military forces and to set limits on their employment. These very substantial powers, particularly the power to appropriate money for military purposes, insure that Congress will always be a key player in foreign policy. No serious enterprise in foreign relations, particularly one that involves the application of military force sustained over time, can hope to succeed unless it rests squarely on informed congressional assent. Whenever presidents ignore this rule, they come to grief. They do not have a constitutionally free hand in the use of military force.

Presidents do not always proceed wisely in foreign relations; neither does Congress. But the system compels them to work together, and it exacts a high price politically from those who try to bypass this requirement for cooperation.

Electoral Disaffection. Some people think that the performance of the electoral system cries out for basic reform. They say that something is fundamentally wrong when less than half of the eligible voters turn out on most election days. They say campaigns are too long and too expensive, that candidates spend too much time raising funds, and in the process sell their allegiance to wealthy interests. Therefore, reforms to give us shorter, cheaper campaigns and a better turnout on election day would draw the American system closer to its democratic ideal.

Defenders of the Constitution make several replies to this line of reformist argument. First, they point out that there are no bars to voting for most citizens. A few potential voters, having recently moved, may fail to meet residency requirements for registration. A few others may be disqualified by reason of incarceration or institutional constraints.

Mostly, however, low turnout results from the free choice of potential voters. Elections are held regularly; they are well publicized; assistance is commonly offered to transport voters to the polling places; voters travelling or on vacation may vote by absentee ballot. In addition, the ballot offers a wide range of choices. If many voters decline to go to the polls, it seems a fair inference that they are satisfied with the results when they don't vote. In other words, non-voting may indicate at least passive consent to the government as it stands.

High turnouts are not always a sign of health in a political system. There was a very high turnout in the elections that signalled Hitler's rise to power in Germany. Dissidents have a right to protest against the existing authorities and to run for office in fair elections, but we ought not to take alarm when they fail to attract a substantial following.

Are campaigns too long? If they are, it is not a recent phenomenon. Andrew Jackson began his successful campaign for the presidency as soon as he was turned aside in 1824. Jefferson's and Lincoln's campaigns lasted several years. Politicians and their aides who are ambitious for the presidency are always plotting and scheming; they go public, whether coyly or blatantly, as soon as it suits their purpose. The media grant their desire for publicity as soon and as long as readers, listeners, or viewers show an interest. Any attempt to regulate this activity violates the most fundamental purpose of the First Amendment, which guards political expressions more jealously than any other kind.

As for the cost of campaigns, those concerns can be met without altering the basic political system. Are campaigns too expensive? What is democracy worth? Do some people and some groups contribute too much? Of course we must prevent government from being "sold" to high bidders. But there are ways to do that without criminalizing the practice of contributing to campaigns.

In reforming the system, we must be particularly careful not to abridge First Amendment freedoms of expression. And bear in mind that the ability of a candidate to raise funds is not irrelevant to his or her fitness as a potential president or member of Congress. It demonstrates organizational capacity and an ability to win the respect of productive citizens.

The Attitude of Blacks

It is worth noting that some of the most dedicated and passionate defenders of the Constitution are black citizens. One might have thought that blacks would be among the critics of the American constitutional and political system, among those most ready to alter a system that held them in slavery for nearly one hundred years, then in subservience for at least another century, and still suffers them to live in the grip of racism.[8]

It ought not to have been surprising, therefore, when Justice Thurgood Marshall, the only descendant of African slaves ever to serve on the United States Supreme Court, recalled this history when he demurred from the Bicentennial celebrations in 1987. It would not do, he said, to praise the founders overmuch. The "wisdom, foresight, and sense of justice exhibited by the Framers," he said, was not "particularly profound." On the contrary, the government they devised was "defective from the start," and it required a civil war, several amendments, and momentous social transformation to set it on the right path. What saved the system was that the meaning of the Constitution was not "forever 'fixed' at the Philadelphia Convention."[9]

Yet Justice Marshall went on to make clear that he was quite comfortable with the constitutional system as it is evolving. He noted that we observe the bicentennial with "hopes not realized and promises not fulfilled." Nevertheless, he uttered no support at all for efforts to revise the system structurally.

Few black thinkers and political leaders go even as far as Justice Marshall in their criticism of the American political system. Blacks in Congress push hard for affirmative-action programs, and Jesse Jackson mobilizes poor blacks and other victims of oppression in support of a movement that seeks radical changes in the domestic and foreign priorities of the government. But structural reforms are not on the agendas of these political movements. On the contrary, reformism is often viewed as a distraction, more the concern of liberals fascinated by the procedures of politics and "good government" than the proper business of those who want to alleviate poverty and develop support for a more humane foreign policy.[10]

Other black leaders, like William Coleman, an attorney who was Secretary of Transportation in President Ford's administration, and Matthew Holden, Jr., professor of political science at the University of Virginia, express skepticism about structural change on grounds that blacks have benefitted from the resistance of the American system to simple majoritarian democracy. It was the non-majoritarian Supreme Court that led the way to the desegregation of schools, and it was the Madisonian system of checks and balances that prevented the conservative movement of the 1980s from dismantling the welfare state. Getting that same system to provide the assistance that many poor people need may be difficult, but a system that responded more sensitively to transient political majorities would not necessarily improve the lot of vulnerable people over the long haul. Better to muddle along with what we've got—after all, it has brought about some pretty solid improvements in the lot of minority people over the years—than to try to "right" ourselves by abolishing forms to which we have grown accustomed.

Better Uses for Reformist Energies

The obstacles to constitutional revision are formidable. We can only assume that revision would take place through one of the procedures for amendment outlined in Article V of the Constitution—that is, through an amendment or set of amendments framed by Congress and ratified by three-quarters of the states; or through amendments developed by a special constitutional convention and then ratified by three-quarters of the states. Either way, amendments must rest on a wide consensus. Small minorities, if they are intensely opposed to change, can block it by entrenching themselves in a few state legislatures. Thus, it was impossible to win ratification for the equal rights amendment, even though 63 percent of the public supported it in surveys of public opinion.[11] How much more difficult would it be to obtain ratification for changes that look disadvantageous or even uncertain from the perspective of a number of entrenched interests?

Reformers sometimes contend that they are aware of these odds, but pursue their speculations because, when the crisis comes, as inevitably it will, they want to be ready with proposals that would make the regime work better, more efficiently and responsibly, without succumbing to tyranny. To this contention, defenders of the system reply that the general public will be no more interested in borrowings from the parliamentary system then than they are now. If and when the roof falls in, Americans will look all the more intently to the structures and processes established in the Constitution as the sheet-anchor of their stability. If they feel compelled in the maelstrom to abandon this tradition, it is unlikely to be in favor of the Westminster model. Nelson Polsby and Aaron Wildavsky add that reforms ride in "on tides of strong feeling. Until such feelings exist among party activists, rational advocacy looking toward reform is wasted; once such feeling exists, rational advocacy is superfluous."[12]

In the meantime, those who are concerned about deficits, the abuse of war powers, and voter apathy might better devote their energies to more conventional political activities. Support candidates who talk sense about fiscal matters. Contribute to the development of a mature and stable public opinion, one that supports a firm foreign policy, but is quick to disapprove of political leaders that go off on crusades.

Remove obstacles that frustrate would-be voters and support candidates and platforms that will draw the widest possible range of potential voters to the polls.

But drop the fantasies about structural reform of the system. It cannot be accomplished, and it is not necessary.

PART THREE

SPECIFIC PROPOSALS

7
How We Choose Our Leaders

COORDINATING THE TERMS OF OFFICE

The Existing Situation

Terms of office for members of the House of Representatives and Senate and for the president and vice-president are fixed in the Constitution (Article I, Section 2; Article I, Section 3; and Article II, Section 1, respectively). A member of the House serves for two years. Each senator serves for six years; he or she is a member of one of three "classes," whose terms end either two years, four years or six years following each national election. A president and vice-president are elected simultaneously; both serve for a term of four years.

The Basic Proposal

RESOLVED: That terms of office for the executive and legislative branches should be coordinated, at least to the extent of providing four-year terms for members of the House, co-terminous with the president's.

Discussion

To change terms of office, it is necessary to amend the Constitution. This proposal would require an amendment of Article I, Section 2, to create four-year terms for House members and cause them to run simultaneously with the president. Even greater coordination could be achieved by extending the terms of senators to eight years and having half of the Senate (one senator from each state) stand for election every four years. In a short-hand version, this arrangement can be called the "4-8-4" option.[1]

If eight years seemed too long for senatorial terms, or if a modified mid-term election seemed desirable, we could extend House terms to four years and leave senatorial terms as they are, at six years: the "4-6-4" option.

Or, if it seemed desirable to put the whole government on a single schedule, we could reduce senators to four-year terms, running simultaneously with the House and president: the "4-4-4" option.

If we thought four years was too long for House members, but still wanted greater cohesion, a mid-term election, and a longer term for presidents, we could extend House terms to three years and presidential terms to six years (with or without a provision that the president not be eligible for reelection), leaving senators' terms at six years, but adjusting the Senate into two "classes" instead of the present three, with each class up for election every three years: the "3-6-6" option.

Note: Some who believe that longer, synchronized terms would be an improvement are unwilling to lengthen terms for House members without incorporating a safety feature. If it were possible to call new elections in the event of a prolonged deadlock or serious scandal short of the full four-year term, it would be less risky to extend House terms. (See the section on dissolution in Chapter 9 and the discussion of possible combinations in Chapter 10.)

Relevant Facts

☐ Proposals to lengthen congressional terms have been introduced in almost every Congress since 1869.[2] Some—including the version favored by President Lyndon Johnson—have provided for House terms synchronized with presidential terms; others—including the proposal that gained greatest support in Congress in the 1960s—would have set House elections during the off-year (thus: presidential elections in 1988 and 1992; House elections in 1990 and 1994).

☐ During the founding period, many people believed that one house of the legislature should have short terms in order to keep the members close to the people. This sentiment was expressed in the aphorism, "Where annual elections end, tyranny begins." Others, however, favored longer terms (three or four years), believing they would encourage greater stability and closer attention to legislative craftsmanship. The provision for a two-year term for members of the House represented a compromise between these positions.

In *The Federalist,* number 52, Madison argued that the House

should have an immediate dependence on, and intimate sympathy with the people. Frequent elections are unquestionably the only policy by which this dependence and sympathy can be effectually secured. But what particular degree of frequency may be absolutely necessary for that purpose, does not appear to be susceptible of any precise calculation. . . . The period of service ought . . . to bear some proportion to the extent of practical knowledge requisite to the due performance of the service.

Some observers believe that the complexity of modern problems requires more "practical knowledge" than during the founding period and justifies longer terms. Others maintain that the speed of modern transportation and communications makes short terms even less of a burden than in the past.

☐ The workload of Congress, as measured by legislative proposals and output, has increased enormously in modern times. In the First Congress (1789–1790), 144 bills were introduced and 118 passed; in the 98th Congress (1983–1984), over 10,000 bills were introduced, of which 491 passed.

☐ Midterm elections almost always diminish the strength of the president's party in Congress. During the 20th century, only in 1934 did the president's party gain members in the House. More typical were the losses of Taft's party in 1910: 10 seats in the Senate and 57 in the House; FDR's in 1938: 6 seats in the Senate, 71 in the House; Lyndon Johnson's in 1966: 4 Senate seats and 47 in the House; and Reagan's in 1986: 8 Senate seats and 5 in the House.

Arguments in Favor of This Proposal

1. Lack of Cohesion. Elected officials at the national level have little sense of shared responsibility. They are not pledged to support a common program, and when they approach issues, they find that other officials are operating on different wave-lengths, not only because they serve different constituencies, but because they face different electoral schedules.

For an elected official, the next election is always a prime consideration in deciding how to act. This is not a matter of self-interest or cynicism. In a democracy, the power of elective office depends on being able to win the election. Presidents and members of Congress are not free to ignore that fact of life.

As their terms begin, members of the House know that they have only a short respite before they must resume campaigning. The president, on the other hand, has four years before he must face the electorate again. And at any given time one-third of the Senate is in the same boat as the whole House, facing a reelection campaign almost immediately; one-third is on the president's schedule; and the other one-third, having just been elected, is secure in office for almost six years.

Thus, in the three centers of political responsibility, elected officials see issues and prospects differently, because they operate on different schedules. The result is a dispersion of outlooks and a tendency toward stalemate, especially when different parties control the White House and one or both houses of Congress.

2. Short Honeymoons. In part because of these differing horizons, new presidential administrations have a very short period—usually no more than a few months[3]—in which they can expect a sympathetic reception for their new initiatives. After that, members of the House and Senate up for reelection will hesitate to support anything bold until they have had a chance to test the popularity of the president's program at the polls.

3. Deadlocks After Midterm. Midterm elections, in every case but one (1934) in the twentieth century, have resulted in reduced majorities in the House for the president's party. That is one reason, as James Sundquist has pointed out, it is difficult to identify "any major new governmental departures," whether progressive or conservative in nature, that occurred "after the midterm election in any administration in this century."[4]

Midterm elections almost always check the progress of the administration, but they cannot remove it from office. Thus, unless the president's term is reduced to two years, which no one has proposed, the midterm election cannot initiate a new order; it can only tend to deadlock the government.

Especially when an administration embarks on a new course, it is premature to ask the electorate to pass judgment after only two years. Would it not be wiser to allow the policies to ripen for a while? By requiring a verdict after just two years, we disrupt the stability and continuity of the government's policies without providing a sound test of their wisdom.

4. Campaigning Versus Governing. Electioneering and governing are two different things. One has an inescapable element of catering to popular prejudices and passions; the other involves tough choices. In the modern era, the range and complexity of public issues is particularly daunting. Legislators need time to master them. It is true, in a democratic regime, that elected officials should face popular judgment on their major decisions, but a wise constitution will give them time to prove the value of their ideas.

5. Longer Terms Mean Better Qualified Candidates. It seems likely that some people who are highly qualified to serve as legislators do not run for a seat in the House because they deplore the constant campaigning. Those currently in the House have presumably come to terms with this demand, but there may be others, with solid aptitude for governing, who would be prepared to campaign on a regular schedule, but who are simply unwilling to spend most of their time on the campaign trail.

6. Fewer Campaigns Mean Lower Costs. Constant campaigning means constant fund-raising, and it favors candidates who are themselves wealthy or who appeal to wealthy people. If there were fewer campaigns, people of more moderate means might be able to afford a campaign, and all candidates would be relieved of the work of fund-raising for at least part of their tenure.

Arguments Against This Proposal

1. Lack of Cohesion. One of the great dangers in democratic politics is that power will be seized by leaders with a single passion and take the nation on a crusade. The framers understood this. That is why they set up staggered elections.[5] Thus, every other time a given seat in Congress, House or Senate comes up for election, it is contested without the distraction of a presidential campaign, so voters in that district or state can concentrate on the local outlook on national issues. This incentive for a local focus is not a mistake. It is part of the framers' design and an important safeguard against majority tyranny.

2. Short Honeymoons. The euphoria that sometimes enables a newly elected president to sweep all opposition before him is dangerous. Factors which stiffen the resistance of Congress should be cherished, not eliminated. This proposal strengthens the presidency too much. By tying congressional elections to the presidential campaign, it would diminish the attention that voters give to congressional races. Presidential coattails would be even more powerful. Many more congressional seats would be vulnerable to sweeping changes led by popular presidential candidates. Members of Congress would have to be sensitive to presidential desires to a degree that would interfere with their responsibility to represent local interests.

3. Deadlocks After Midterm. Party cohesion and the results it can produce in terms of governmental programs are less important than a legislator's independence and responsiveness to his or her constituency.

4. Campaigning Versus Governing. The House of Representatives is the people's chamber. It is "close to the people." The longer terms for senators and presidents insure that the federal government will have the wisdom that comes from detachment. But it is essential that part of the system be closely tethered to the wisdom that comes from engagement in the concrete affairs of common people. Besides, many House members come from "safe" districts. These members are "safe" because they faithfully represent their constituents, but most of them do not have to spend a lot of time electioneering.

5. Longer Terms Mean Better Qualified Candidates. Very few members of the House retire voluntarily after brief service. Most quit, not because of the strain and cost of biennial elections, but because of death, defeat (or the fear of it), or ambition for higher office. Sundquist, who has been a close observer of the political culture of Capitol Hill for over four decades, concludes, "House members find their careers satisfying and attractive despite the two-year term."[6]

As for those who are discouraged by the two-year term from ever entering national politics, how many are there? If they are put off by the need to campaign, they cannot truly be qualified for service in a democratic legislature.

6. Fewer Campaigns Mean Lower Costs. Fund-raising is an integral part of democratic politics. It shows that a candidate is well-organized and ties him or her to the concerns of productive people. Furthermore, contributing to campaigns is an important way of participating in politics. The cost of frequent elections is the price we pay for a responsive legislature. If we are concerned about abuses in campaign financing, there are better ways of getting at them than by extending House terms.

Besides, fund-raising is often preemptive. Candidates try to intimidate potential opponents by accumulating huge war-chests. Many senators, with six-year terms, begin raising funds for the next campaign from the moment of their election. Extending House terms would be unlikely to cause members to devote less time to fund-raising or spend less on their campaigns.

You Decide

☐ Is it important to increase the cohesion of the government and lengthen the period of its productivity, even at the cost of sacrificing some of the responsiveness of Congress to local interests?

☐ How likely is it that the electorate will be swept away by momentary passions? If we chose the president and the whole Congress simultaneously, would there be danger that voters would give impetus to foolish plans?

☐ Would coordinated terms give too much power to the president, whose campaign is likely to draw the greatest national attention?

☐ Are we ill-served by an electoral cycle that keeps members of the House campaigning for reelection all the time? Would longer terms relieve the pressure of constant campaigning? Would they enable members of the House to take a more statesmanlike approach?

☐ Would it be dangerous to have the government locked in place for four years, with no midterm election to gauge popular sentiments?

ENCOURAGING PARTY SLATES

The Existing Situation

By the Constitution, state legislatures normally establish the form of the ballot for congressional (Article I, Section 4) and presidential (Article II, Section 1) elections. However, the Constitution provides that Congress, if it chooses, may enact regulations for congressional elections. Congress has in fact passed a number of statutes regulating federal elections. For example, there are federal laws governing the financing of national campaigns[7], outlawing discrimination at local polling places, and assigning federal officials to serve as voting registrars.

Thus, Congress already regulates elections in many ways. The question in this section is: Should there be additional regulations designed specifically to encourage political parties?

The Basic Proposal

RESOLVED: That we should encourage party discipline and responsibility by providing voters with the option of voting for a straight party ticket for federal offices.

Possible Variations

☐ We could discourage ticket-splitting by requiring every state to give voters the option to vote for a straight party ticket. The effect would be that a voter, by casting his or her vote for a party slate, would give one vote to each candidate—for president, vice-president, senator (if a senate seat was at stake that year in the voter's state) and representative—nominated by that party for federal office.[8]

☐ If we were determined to prevent ticket-splitting completely, we could adopt a constitutional amendment requiring that voters in each federal election be presented with a ballot containing slates listing each party's nominees for all federal offices. Voters would then choose between these partisan slates, rather than voting for individual candidates for particular offices.[9]

Because two-thirds of the Senate seats would not be at stake in any given election year, it would still be possible, even with this amendment mandating straight-ticket voting, to have the administration controlled by one party and one house of Congress (the Senate) by the other. Also, it would be mathematically possible, because of the electoral college, for one party to win the most House seats, while the other party won the presidency.[10] But a constitutionally mandated "team ticket" would reduce that possibility to a minimum.

Relevant Facts

☐ For one hundred years beginning in 1854 (the birth of the Republican Party), only twice did incoming presidents face either house of Congress under the control of the opposition party: Rutherford B. Hayes in 1877 faced a Democratic House (his opponent, Samuel Tilden, had won the popular vote), and Grover Cleveland began his first term in 1885 with a Republican Senate. In twelve other cases, the mid-term election gave control of at least one house to the opposition party. Nevertheless, through Eisenhower's first term, a president could normally count on having members of his party control both chambers of Congress, at least through his first two years in office.[11]

Since 1954, however, divided government has become the norm. From Eisenhower's inauguration through Bush's first term (40 years), we will have had divided government almost two-thirds of the time (26 years; 65 percent of the time). Three presidents during these four decades (Nixon, Reagan and Bush, not to mention Ford, who came to office under special circumstances) began their terms facing at least one house of Congress dominated by the opposition party.

☐ The recent increase in the incidence of "divided government" is a product of Republican victories in the race for the presidency, coupled with continuing Democratic control of the House of Representatives. Democratic control of the House results at least partly from inertia. During the past 40 years (since 1950), over ninety percent of incumbents seeking reelection have won in all but four national elections, and in two of those (1964 and 1974) the defeat of incumbents resulted in strengthening the Democratic hold. The other two were 1958, when 89.9 percent of incumbents who sought reelection were successful, and 1966, when the Republicans regained some of the staggering losses of 1964.[12] If the ballot successfully discouraged ticket-splitting during this period, it might well have meant Republican victories in congressional races (on the coattails of Eisenhower, Nixon and Reagan), rather than Democratic victories in the race for the presidency.

☐ As Chapter 2 of this book makes clear, the adoption of the so-called Australian ballot (printed by the government, listing all duly nominated candidates, and cast in secret) may have cleaned up the electoral process, but it also deprived parties of an important function (printing and distributing ballots). Some states went further and adopted the office-block ballot, grouping candidates, not under separate columns for each party, but according to the office they sought. Thus, if a voter wanted to support a straight party ticket, he or she had to search for the Republican or Democratic candidate, listed in random order, for each office. And in at least one state (Virginia), party designations are not even indicated on the ballot.

Not all states have carried "reform" to this extreme. Nineteen states, including Illinois, New York and Pennsylvania, still give voters the option of casting a straight party ballot. However, research by James Sundquist suggests that ticket-splitting has been no less common in those states than in states that do not provide this option.[13]

☐ Divided government is produced by a minority of voters who split their tickets. In the two recent elections with the greatest proportion of ticket-splitting (1972 and 1984), 56 percent of the congressional districts in each contest (243 out of 435) returned majorities for the candidates of the same party. Even within the districts that produced split results, only a minority of voters cast split ballots.

The 1972 election was an extreme example of ticket-splitting. In that contest, Nixon ran 15 percentage points ahead of the Republican House candidates. If as many as 5 percent voted for George McGovern and for Republican congressional candidates (probably a generous assumption), then 20 percent must have switched the other way to give Nixon his net margin of 15 percent. Thus, only 25 percent in 1972 split their tickets. It was this minority of the electorate that gave us divided government.[14]

Polls done in 1984—another year of extreme ticket-splitting—show a similar pattern. President Reagan, the Republican nominee, won by 59 percent to 41 percent, while Democratic candidates for Congress were outdrawing their Republican opponents by 55 percent to 45 percent. Yet interviews conducted by the Survey Research Center indicated that only about one-quarter of the voters split their ticket:

19.6 percent who voted for Reagan and the Democratic candidate for Congress, and 5.6 percent for Walter Mondale and a Republican for Congress. That left three-quarters of the electorate (74.6 percent) who voted straight tickets that year.

In most contests since 1954, the minority of ticket-splitters was even smaller. Exit polls in 1988—when President Bush won by about 55 percent, while Democratic candidates for Congress received about 53 percent of votes cast in their races—indicate that fewer than 20 percent of all voters split their tickets for federal candidates. In other words, over 80 percent voted a straight ticket.[15]

Arguments in Favor of This Proposal

1. Divided Government and Reformist Efforts. As the facts here show, divided government is a relatively recent phenomenon. It is the fruit of a series of assaults on parties by Progressive reformers and, especially since mid-century, of technological developments that have undermined the role that parties play in our system of governance. We should stop taking parties for granted. Reformers of this generation, recognizing that parties are essential to democratic politics, should take steps that fortify them for the role they play.

2. The Cost of Divided Government. The problems we face are difficult enough without the added bitterness of partisan conflict built into the very structure of government. Our constitutional system separates the executive and legislative powers and enables them to check one another. When those branches are controlled by different parties, healthy surveillance often degenerates into raucous, boring, and unproductive stalemate.

Parties are naturally combative. When partisan wars are entrenched in the institutional structure of the government, a bitter deadlock tends to result. Richard Nixon declares in his memoirs that, as he began his second term, he "threw down a gauntlet to Congress, the bureaucracy, the media, and the Washington establishment and challenged them to epic battle."[16] Congress stepped up to the challenge and finally drove Nixon from office, but at enormous cost to the effectiveness of government.

Most confrontations between the branches are less dramatic than that, but periods of fruitless conflict are typical during periods of divided government. During Gerald Ford's brief tenure, for example, Congress sought to take control of foreign policy, thwarting the president's initiatives toward the Soviet Union, Cyprus and Angola; meanwhile, the president exercised his veto seventy-two times, blocking nearly every important measure that Congress tried to enact. Dwight

Eisenhower had greater success in foreign policy, but domestically his tenure was marked by maneuvering with a Congress controlled by the Democrats.[17] The Reagan administration, after a remarkable burst of achievement in the first year, also got bogged down in a pattern of partisan sniping, particularly in domestic policy. When the Democrats regained control of the Senate in the 1986 elections, any realistic hope for measures to straighten out the government's fiscal mess vanished.

3. The Preferences of Voters. As the facts above make clear, the recent string of divided governments does not represent the will and judgment of the American people. It represents the preferences of a minority of voters, whose decision to split their tickets, in a closely competitive, two-party system, results in divided government.

4. The Ethos of Teamwork. Americans are deeply committed to checks and balances. But we also value teamwork. Government cannot achieve great ends when its members are perpetually antagonistic.

No one wants Congress to be a rubber-stamp in the hands of the administration. But if Congress is to play its role as partner in the formulation of foreign and domestic policies, there must be a measure of trust and shared purpose between members of the two branches.

If the electoral fates of the president and Congress were more closely linked, legislators of the president's party would want to support his program and help him succeed. They would know that, if he failed, they would suffer at the polls with him. On the other hand, if his policies seemed unwise or his performance in office was drawing widespread criticism, they would pressure him to set a new course.

5. The Form of the Ballot. If federal law required all states to provide the opportunity to vote a straight ticket by making just one mark, voters would still be free to split their ticket if they desired, but they could also vote for party government if that was their preference. It would increase the voter's options.

6. The Clarity of Electoral Verdicts. When government is divided, voters cannot render a clear verdict on its performance. Whose fault is it that the budget deficit rose so sharply during the 1980s? The Republican president said he knew how to curb it, but the Democratic Congress would not cooperate. Congress blamed the president. Given the partisan division within the government, there was no way for voters to discipline either party or to indicate a preferred course of action for correcting the problem. Unless we can somehow discourage ticket-splitting, the vicious circle of divided governments and muddled mandates will continue unbroken.

7. Tradition and Expectation. We already use a team ticket for president and vice-president. Voters in 1988 could not support George Bush and Lloyd Bentsen, or Michael Dukakis and J. Danforth Quayle; they had to support one ticket or the other. If it is feasible for the executive branch, is it not worth considering a team approach throughout the government?

8. The Prospects for a Mandatory Straight-Ticket Amendment. It would indeed be difficult to persuade members of Congress to support an amendment mandating a straight party vote for candidates in both the executive and legislative branches. They would be most reluctant to tie their electoral fate so closely to the presidential race.

But if we became convinced that it was a good idea despite this opposition, it might be necessary to pursue the amendment through the alternative method provided in Article V of the Constitution (calling a special convention to work out a proposal; see Chapter 11 of this book). The framers provided this alternative route for just such situations as this: where Congress, for reasons of self-preservation, might block a reform that would benefit the rest of the system.

Arguments Against This Proposal

1. Divided Government and Reformist Efforts. The recent inclination toward divided government reflects the voters' preference for Republican presidential candidates and their loyalty to their present representatives in Congress. Those who favor party government should work to improve their party's nominees and performance in campaigns, instead of inventing new straitjackets for voters.

2. The Cost of Divided Government. Bipartisan governments are not always stalemated. The postwar foreign policy of containment was set in the late 1940s by the brilliant collaboration of the Truman administration and Republican leaders in Congress. When broad popular support exists, even a divided government can build strong policies.

As for the instances of stalemate, often they arise from congressional resistance to misguided efforts by the administration. An independent Congress served the nation well by ferreting out the truth about Watergate and bringing the obstructors to justice. A decade later, Congress again played a crucial role in preventing the Reagan administration from undermining civil rights and dismantling the social security system.

3. The Preferences of Voters. Evidence indeed shows that most voters tend to support one party or the other for all national offices. But the crucial thing is that they be free to choose, without pressure or coercion.

4. The Ethos of Teamwork. Americans love teamwork, but polls show that they are deeply suspicious of parties.[18] Parties play a useful role in our system, but they are also full of mischief and corruption. The reform of parties—the effort of civic groups to block their attempts to secure power—has been one of the primary themes of 20th century political history in America. Primaries took the control of nominations from bosses. Nonpartisan municipal elections took city governments away from the parties. Civil service countered the patronage system. Public financing of campaigns made candidates less dependent on party machinery to raise funds.

The Australian ballot is part of this pattern. The mandatory team ticket would reverse it, and so, to a lesser extent, would the enactment of federal legislation requiring states to facilitate a vote for a party slate.

5. The Form of the Ballot. In fact, the party-slate option at the state level has made very little, if any, difference. James Sundquist has shown that the spread between presidential and senatorial candidates in states having the straight-ticket option is only slightly lower than in states not having the option (an average of 8.2 percent as compared with 10.9 percent in the 1980 election), and the proportion of split outcomes was about the same. In 1980, despite the straight-ticket option, Democratic Senators Christopher Dodd of Connecticut, Alan Dixon of Illinois, Wendell Ford of Kentucky, Tom Eagleton of Missouri and Ernest Hollings of South Carolina survived the Reagan tide in their states. In 1984, states with a straight-ticket option actually showed a higher percentage of split outcomes in senatorial races than states without it.[19]

6. The Clarity of Electoral Verdicts. Unambiguous electoral verdicts are still possible, when the national mind is made up. The verdict on the Carter administration in 1980, for example, was pretty clear. The failure to render judgment on budget deficits probably stems from a popular feeling that it does not matter very much, or that it is not clear how best to deal with it. During the heyday of divided governments (mid-1950s to the present), there was a clear mandate in 1964, and to a lesser extent in 1980, and in both cases, the government moved swiftly and effectively to implement it. In the other cases, the electorate was simply not ready to give a clear mandate, and an electoral system that rendered a decisive verdict in these circumstances would not have been truly representative.

7. *Tradition and Expectation.* The comparison with the presidential ticket is false. The American tradition strongly supports a clear separation between the executive and legislative branches, and the American people want an electoral system that reflects that separation. In polls taken during the 1984 campaign, for example, by majorities of 55 and 60 percent in two different samples, respondents asserted that the country would be "worse off" if President Reagan had "a Republican-controlled Congress that would pass nearly everything he wants."[20]

8. *The Prospects for a Mandatory Straight-Ticket Amendment.* The traditional method of amending the Constitution is for proposals to pass through Congress (by two-thirds majorities in each house) and then be ratified by three-quarters of the states. Members of Congress would be highly unlikely to support a constitutional amendment mandating a "team ticket." Most members of Congress, in both houses, have survived an election in which they won despite the victory, in their state or district, of the presidential nominee of the opposite party. In these circumstances, members would have to believe very strongly in the principle of party government in order to support an amendment that might well drag them down to defeat in due course.

You Decide

☐ Is divided government (with the presidency and at least one house of Congress dominated by opposite parties) a problem or not? Would the government be more effective if both branches were controlled by the same party?

☐ Would it be easier for the electorate to render a clear verdict on governmental performance if both branches were controlled by the same party? Or do the system's checks and balances work better if Congress is controlled by the opposite party?

☐ If divided government is a problem, is it serious enough to justify the team-ticket approach, either as an option or in a ballot that gave voters no choice?

CAPPING EXPENDITURES IN CONGRESSIONAL CAMPAIGNS

The Existing Situation

Currently, there is no limit on the amount of money that a candidate may spend on a campaign for the House or Senate. The Supreme Court ruled in 1976 (*Buckley vs. Valeo*) that legislated ceilings on overall campaign expenditures violate the First Amendment's guarantee of free speech.

Federal law does limit contributions to political campaigns by individuals or organized groups, including political action committees, or PACs (see Relevant Facts, below, for details). Citing the constitutional guarantee of equal protection, the Supreme Court upheld these limits, although an exception was made for contributions in any amount by the candidate him- or herself, or by a candidate's immediate family. These, said the Court, are protected by the First Amendment.

For similar reasons (that is, on First Amendment grounds), the Court has found that a candidate's overall campaign expenditures may not be limited. Money buys expression. By the Court's reasoning, if we limit the money that a campaign organization can spend, we inhibit the expression of political ideas.

Therefore, by prevailing constitutional interpretation, we cannot put a ceiling on overall expenditures in a campaign for Congress.

The Basic Proposal

RESOLVED: That we need to set effective limits on spending for congressional campaigns.

Discussion

Assuming that the Supreme Court adheres to its 1976 ruling, there are two ways to limit campaign spending: by amending the Constitution, or by inducing candidates or political parties to set limits on themselves.

A constitutional amendment could supercede the Court's decision by giving Congress power to set reasonable limits on campaign spending. Once the amendment was adopted, Congress could implement it by legislation that applied to both primary and general elections, setting limits adjusted to the population of districts and states.

Another approach would be to use party rules. For various reasons, including the difficulty of amending the Constitution, some people believe that we should try to induce the parties to impose limits on themselves.

One proposal would have a political party resolve to restrict the size of individual contributions that its candidates could accept and set an overall ceiling on the amount its candidates could spend in their campaigns for Congress. Under this proposal, all contributions made in support of a campaign, whether for the party's nomination or for the general campaign, would be sent to the party treasurer and held in an account for the candidate's use. Disbursements would be made, at the direction of the candidate, in accordance with the limits established by the party's rules. The party would establish a special committee to oversee the administration of these rules, and the committee would adopt procedures for investigating complaints and would have authority to impose sanctions for violations.

There would be various ways for the parties to proceed in implementing such a system of voluntary restraints. The Republican and Democratic National Committees could establish a joint, bipartisan commission to formulate rules for campaign spending. Or one party could develop a set of guidelines and commit itself to abide by them if the other party would make a similar commitment. Another idea would be to apply the rules to its own candidates and make a political issue of it if the other party refused to join the accord.

Or it might be possible for one or more private organizations (the League of Women Voters? Common Cause?), separately or together, to develop guidelines on campaign spending and induce the parties to accept them. In Great Britain, so-called "royal commissions," appointed by the government, are sometimes able to clarify and articulate a public demand for reform. In America, specially appointed, bi-partisan groups developed proposals on social security reform and the siting of MX missiles. Perhaps a similar body could lend weight to the call for campaign spending reforms.

Relevant Facts

☐ To run for a seat in Congress is expensive almost beyond imagination. In 1986, in California, the two major party candidates for senator each spent over $11 million; in Florida that year, the two candidates for senator spent $6 million each. A candidate in New York state spent $6 million in a losing effort to win the Democratic nomination in his party's primary. Even in relatively "small" states, candidates spent huge sums on their campaigns. The losing candidate in Idaho, a Democrat, spent $2.1 million in 1986; the losing candidate in Vermont, a Republican, spent $1.5 million.

For House seats, the totals in 1986 were generally lower, but still huge. Jack Kemp amassed a war-chest of $2.6 million to win reelection in upstate New York. Young Joe Kennedy spent $1.8 million to win Tip O'Neill's seat in Cambridge, Massachusetts. Bella Abzug plunked down $900,000 in Westchester County, New York, and lost. Dick Gephardt spent nearly $900,000 to win in suburban St. Louis.

These were not unusual cases. There were over 50 candidates for House seats who spent in excess of $700,000 on their races in 1986. A similar list for the Senate showed fifty candidates who spent over $1.3 million on his or her campaign that year.

☐ Under current law, individuals must limit their political contributions overall to $25,000 per year and may contribute no more than $1000 to any House or Senate candidate (that is, $1000 each for the primary, runoff and general election campaigns). Also, each PAC is limited to $5,000 in contributions to any candidate for House or Senate for each race (that is, primary, run-off and general elections).

☐ Since the beginning of the twentieth century, there have been a number of efforts to set limits on contributions and overall campaign spending. For example, a law passed in 1907 prohibited contributions by corporations to candidates for federal office, and the Taft-Hartley Act of 1947 extended the ban to labor unions. Both interests, however, easily found ways to provide funds to their favorites through indirect channels. Similarly, the Hatch Act of 1940 limited an individual's contribution to a federal candidate to $5000, but wealthy people circumvented the law by making additional contributions to various campaign committees.

Hearings on the Watergate scandal of the early 1970s gave impetus to the drive for reform by revealing some whopping contributions to the Nixon and McGovern campaigns in 1972 and detailing a virtual auction of presidential appointments by Nixon's staff. Public outrage led to the passage of a wide-ranging package of reforms in 1974. However, as noted above, the Supreme Court in 1976 declared several of these measures unconstitutional—particularly those that imposed ceilings on candidates' contributions to their own campaigns and those that set overall ceilings on campaign expenditures.

The reforms of the early 1970s had the ironic effect of stimulating the proliferation of PACs. There were 113 PACs in 1971; by 1983, there were 3,525. In the mid-1970s, PACs contributed about $12 million to congressional candidates; by 1982, over $87 million went to congressional campaigns. PAC contributions provided over 25 percent of overall congressional campaign spending that year.

Arguments in Favor of This Proposal

1. Free Expression. To break the logjam created by the Court's decision in the *Buckley* case, we need a constitutional amendment that enables Congress to stop the auctioning of seats in Congress. Reasonable limits on campaign spending would not endanger the free expression of political ideas. Their effect would be to prevent rich politicians, or those who serve the rich, from overwhelming less well-endowed candidates.

2. Equity. Ceilings imposed by Congress or by the parties can be set high enough to permit strong campaigns by both challengers and incumbents. Such ceilings would prevent the buying of a seat in Congress by PACs and other well-heeled groups and wealthy individuals.

3. Influence of Wealth. Americans, it is said, have "the best Congress money can buy." Elections ought not to be decided by money. When they are, the constitutional guarantee of equal protection is mocked.

The problem is not that we spend too much overall on campaigning. As a nation, we spend more on cosmetics, pet food and power lawn mowers than we do on political campaigns. The problem is that certain candidates are able to amass great war-chests and thereby frighten off or overwhelm potential opposition.

4. Enforceability. The Federal Election Commission has been a disappointment to those who hoped it would bring strong, independent leverage to bear on the electoral process. Its budget is severely limited, and its disclosures of campaign spending are often so detailed and tardy that they have little impact.

5. Influence on Party Control. The plan outlined here for party self-regulation would strengthen the party's leverage in dealing with its candidate-members. Both the requirement that contributions pass through the party treasury and the spending limits, reducing the importance of individual wealth and fund-raising efforts, would link candidates more closely to the party structure than currently is the case.

Arguments Against This Proposal

1. Free Expression. The Court was right in 1976: Any legislated ceiling on campaign expenditures would inhibit free expression in the political arena. Limitations on overall spending would soon lead to restrictions on the substance of the campaign. We ought not to start down that road. Political competition should not be regulated. Voters must be the judges of acceptable conduct and punish breaches at the polls.

2. Equity. Ceilings on campaign spending are inherently inequitable. It costs a lot of money to dislodge an incumbent. If the ceilings were set low enough to suit candidates of modest means, they would protect incumbents; if not, they would be meaningless.

3. Influence of Wealth. Attempts to impose ceilings on campaign spending are unfair. They are thinly disguised attempts to take away the advantage that rightly belongs to the party that has been more successful in raising funds. It makes sense to limit the contributions of wealthy individuals and well endowed groups, as the law now does. But a party ought not to be penalized because it has shown the energy and commitment to hustle for the money it needs to conduct a strong campaign.

4. Enforceability. Ceilings invite evasion. Look at what has happened to presidential campaigns. The huge grants ($40 million in 1988) for general campaigns are now supplemented by funds raised and spent by "independent committees," and the parties themselves supplement their candidates' efforts by "soft money," raised and spent for such purposes as registration drives by state parties.

When money can be raised for political purposes, campaign officials will find a way to spend it, but there is nothing to regret about this fact of political life. Money draws people into the political arena; it encourages broad participation. It is foolish and counter-productive, from the standpoint of democratic values, to try to restrict it.

5. Influence on Party Control. Allowing the party hierarchy to have command over all campaign funds puts the fox in charge of the chicken coop. It would also centralize politics in a way that is contrary to American traditions of representation.

You Decide

☐ Can we set a limit on money spent in political campaigns without interfering with freedom of expression?

☐ Should we amend the Constitution for this purpose, or would it be better to try to accomplish the same result through voluntary compacts between the parties and candidates?

PROVIDING PUBLIC FUNDS FOR CONGRESSIONAL CAMPAIGNS

The Existing Situation

The federal government currently provides funds to candidates and parties for the presidential campaign, but none for congressional campaigns.

In the presidential campaign, the government matches funds raised by candidates in the primaries. To qualify for these matching funds, a candidate in the 1988 presidential primaries had to raise $5000 in small donations in each of twenty different states. (Only $250 of any individual's contribution could be counted toward this minimum.) With these matching funds, candidates had to accept a set of limits on spending, including $27.7 million of total expenditures during the pre-nomination campaign and limits on spending in specific states (in

1988, $461,000 in New Hampshire, for example, and $7.5 million in California).

After the conventions choose their nominees for president and vice-president, the government gives each major party several million dollars (in 1988, $40 million), with the understanding that the parties will not raise or spend any additional money on the presidential campaign. In this way, the government's support is intended to operate as a ceiling on expenditures for the presidential campaign.

The Supreme Court has confirmed these arrangements for presidential campaigns, though it did strike down the law's limit on contributions by a candidate to his or her own campaign. Also, in 1985, the Supreme Court struck down legislation that limited the amount that an "independent committee" could spend in support of a presidential candidate. (A committee is considered independent so long as there is no cooperation with any candidate or organization in planning its activities.)

The Basic Proposal

RESOLVED: That the government should provide public funds to support campaigns for seats in the House and Senate.

Discussion

The idea behind this proposal is to provide public financing for congressional campaigns, so that incumbents who seek reelection and their opponents would have sufficient money to mount decent campaigns without having to rely on well-heeled special interests.

Possible Variations

☐ Noting that expenditures for television advertising are often the largest single element in the cost of campaigns for Congress, the Committee on the Constitutional System has offered a version of this proposal that focuses on media expenditures. The CCS proposal would create a Congressional Campaign Broadcast Fund, funded out of general revenues or by an optional contribution marked on income tax returns. The money would be distributed, half to party committees and half directly to candidates who have won major party nominations, on condition that neither the committees nor the candidates spend any other money on campaign broadcasts. The half that went to the party committees could be spent only on broadcasts related to the congressional campaign. Parties would presumably spend these funds in a way that would maximize the party's chance to win (or increase) a majority in Congress.

The CCS version is designed to achieve two purposes: to provide adequate funds for a major part of the cost of congressional campaigns; and to strengthen parties as a force for coherence in the political system. Those who do not favor the latter goal could design the statute to distribute all of the money directly to the candidates, rather than half of it to partisan committees.

☐ One problem with legislation of this kind is the treatment of independents and minor party candidates. The law might allow such candidates to share in the distribution if they obtained a certain number of signatures, or if the party's candidate had polled a certain proportion of votes in a preceding election, or if the candidate won a certain proportion of the vote in the election in question. The aim would be to support candidates that had some real popular support, without spending public funds on campaigns designed primarily to promote the name of the candidate.

☐ The proposed statute would cover general elections only. It might be possible to make money available for primary campaigns, too, though it would not be easy for the law to define the qualifications of a truly competitive candidate, so as to avoid spending public funds on quixotic efforts. Perhaps the law on funding presidential campaigns could be a model.

☐ In providing money for campaign broadcasts, the statute could attempt at the same time to raise the quality of information in political advertising over radio and television. Following the example of other democracies that have established regulations for the benefit of voters, the statute might set a minimum length for such broadcasts (five minutes?), or it might require live appearances by the candidate him- or herself in each broadcast. The former provision is based on the notion that it is more difficult to sustain a crude appeal to prejudice for several minutes than to insinuate it in repeated, brief messages. The latter requirement (live appearances) might favor candidates with professional training in the entertainment arts.

Relevant Facts

☐ Money in a campaign goes for public opinion polling, telephone banks, and computers (including the time of those who know how to use these technologies), and for printing and postage. But above all, in many districts and states, it goes for television and radio advertising. Herbert Alexander, one of the most careful students of campaign finance, has written, "The quantum jump in campaign spending that began in the 1950s can be attributed in considerable measure to the use of television."[21]

In 1984, the average cost for a one-minute commercial on a local television station was $1,500. And before a candidate buys the time, he or she must plan a media campaign (consultants in this field usually charge at least $500 per day), hire equipment and technicians, and rent a studio.

□ A recent survey of twenty democratic countries around the world showed that only four of them (Australia, Canada, Japan and the United States) *permitted* paid political advertising on television. In all but three (Norway, Sri Lanka, and the United States), time on television was given to political parties free of charge during election campaigns.[22]

In most constitutional democracies (France, West Germany, Great Britain, India, Ireland, Italy, Spain, Sweden, and seven others), candidates are forbidden to buy television advertising for themselves, but the laws provide candidates and political parties with free television time for campaign broadcasts.

□ When Senator Robert Byrd, Democrat of West Virginia, was the Senate Majority Leader (through 1988), he championed a bill that would have provided public financing for Senate candidates who agreed voluntarily to abide by certain limits in primary and general election races. The bill would have limited the amount that a candidate could accept from a political action committee (PAC). Byrd said that his principal concern was that senators were spending too much of their time raising campaign funds.

□ Historically, efforts to reform campaign financing in the U.S. have usually centered on setting a *ceiling* on contributions and expenditures. (See the previous section for discussion of a proposal to put an effective ceiling on campaign expenditures.) The idea of putting a *floor* under competitive congressional campaigns, through public financing, goes back to the Progressive Era (around the turn into the twentieth century), but it never came close to enactment until the Watergate hearings revealed the link between campaign contributions and the allocation of favors and appointments. In 1974, Congress enacted public financing for presidential campaigns. At the same time, a bill to provide public funds for congressional campaigns passed the Senate, but failed in the House by 41 votes. The 1974 bill was different from what is proposed here: It would have given all of the money directly to candidates (rather than to party committees); it would not have been limited in purpose (to broadcast advertising); and the funds could have been claimed, on a matching-fund basis, by any candidate, not just those nominated by major parties.[23]

Arguments in Favor of This Proposal

1. Value of Fundraising. To win a seat in Congress under existing conditions, one must be either personally wealthy or willing to satisfy the demands of well-heeled special interests. This proposal, by guaranteeing support for broadcasting a candidate's basic message, would enable a person of modest means to mount a decent campaign without having first to raise enormous amounts of money.

2. Expense. Whatever it cost the federal treasury, it would be money well spent. If we can afford over one trillion dollars annually for other purposes, we can afford the relatively small amount of money it costs to make Congress honest, weaken the disproportionate influence of wealthier citizens, and restore competition to our politics.

3. Influence of Outsiders. Often a candidate is forced to look outside his or her own district or state in order to raise funds to run for Congress. When this happens, voters in the district lose influence over their own representative. This proposal would make it less necessary for candidates to forage for funds outside his or her own district or state.

4. Incumbency. The rate of reelection for incumbents is astonishingly high—well over 95 percent in recent House elections. Many incumbents run virtually unopposed. An incumbent has many advantages: a large staff, the franking privilege,[24] name-recognition, the ability to command time on news broadcasts. And there is a vicious circle, too: Groups that must deal with Congress are reluctant to antagonize a likely winner by helping his or her opponent.

It is no remedy for this situation to put a ceiling on campaign expenditures. Often a challenger must outspend the incumbent to have any chance of winning. The best remedy is to provide all legitimate candidates (that is, those with a decent chance of gaining substantial support among the voters) with adequate means of getting their message out to the voters.

5. Constitutionality. The Supreme Court has struck down a number of efforts to put a cap on campaign expenditures, on grounds that they threaten one of the most basic guarantees of the First Amendment: the right to communicate a political message. But the Court has accepted the basic principle of the 1974 legislation, which provides funds for the presidential campaign: The law may demand that those who accept public funds must not raise or spend any other funds. Requiring such a promise seems to be the only permissible way to limit campaign spending, short of adopting a constitutional amendment that establishes the right of Congress to set reasonable limits on campaign expenditures.

6. *Regulating the Messages.* Perhaps we should tie other conditions to the acceptance of this money (see the last point under Possible Variations, above). Television and radio advertising is often negative and emotionally charged, and it tends to deal in rapid-fire images, rather than the information voters need to make up their minds about the character and commitments of the candidates.

Campaigns are not seminars. Passions are an integral part of politics. But if campaign broadcasts had to be of a certain length, and if candidates had always to appear live and in person, such broadcasts might be more likely to serve the interests of voters, as well as candidates. In framing this legislation, Congress ought to invite testimony from media experts, both domestic and foreign, about how to set these standards.

7. *Party Cohesion.* Giving half of the funds to party committees is a way of strengthening the parties. If party committees distributed half of the funds, they would presumably put them where they would do the most good—into races where an infusion of funds might enable them to win a close seat. In such a case, the winner would have a strong incentive to support his party in Congress.

8. *Effectiveness of Limits.* While it is true that spending got out of hand in 1988, we ought not to abandon the effort. What we need is more resolute enforcement, and perhaps some legislative amendments to clarify and strengthen the will to cap spending.

Arguments Against This Proposal

1. *Value of Fundraising.* Raising campaign funds is a legitimate part of running for Congress. If most of a candidate's funding comes from the federal treasury, we will lose one of the most powerful ties that bind a member to his or her district.

Until a would-be candidate has raised some funds, he or she knows very little of what politics in this country is all about. Legislation almost always involves the regulation of property. Those who aspire to write laws ought to know, or learn, something about the concerns of those who control the society's wealth.

2. *Expense.* A program like the one outlined here would be extremely expensive. If we gave $100,000 for radio and television advertising to

two major-party candidates in each House district, it would cost over $86 million. Beyond that, the CCS version provides a similar amount to the party committees. Grants for the senatorial campaigns would presumably be pro-rated to the population of the states; they, too, would consume a great deal of money. Do we really want to devote a half-billion dollars of public funds every two years to the enrichment of people who make and broadcast media advertising?

3. Influence of Outsiders. Wherever a candidate raises his or her funds, it is the voters in the district who determine who wins a congressional election. If a candidate is "bought" by interests outside the district, let the opponent raise that issue, and let the voters decide.

4. Incumbency. It is true that incumbents have won many recent elections. But that is probably because people are generally satisfied with the state of the nation. If discontent were widespread and voters were looking for alternatives, serious opposition would arise and incumbency would be no advantage.

5. Constitutionality. This legislation would raise very serious constitutional problems, however it is phrased. It is not clear that the Supreme Court would tolerate any scheme designed to control the amount of political advertising. It is particularly dubious that the Court would permit guidelines relating to the content of such messages.

There is a problem, too, about the size of the grants. If they were too large, the Court might find that they coerced candidates to yield their freedom of expression; if they were small enough to avoid this criticism, wealthy candidates might reject them and the limits that went with them.

6. Regulating the Messages. Even if it survives constitutional scrutiny, this law would be bad policy. The temptation to load it with "guidelines" about the format of political broadcasts would be irresistible, even though it is foolish to try to legislate virtue in political combat.

We show a patronizing attitude toward voters when we start to regulate in this fashion. Ultimately the best discipline for political advertisers is the response of voters. If a campaign transgresses the bounds of decency, voters will be repelled. It is the culture—ultimately the voters—who determine what is decent.

7. Party Cohesion. This measure would do very little to encourage party cohesion. A party's committee will support the candidate who has the best chance of winning the district or state, whether or not he is loyal to the party's platform. Senator Jesse Helms may infuriate a lot of national Republicans, but it would be suicide for a Republican committee to support another candidate against him in North Carolina.

Besides, even if a party's funding encourages loyalty, do we really want members forced to toe the party line from fear of being cut off next time? That is contrary to the American idea of representation, where control lies in the district, not in a central party committee.

8. *Effectiveness of Limits.* Recent experience in presidential campaigns shows that campaign spending cannot be limited by making grants conditional on an agreement not to spend other funds. For awhile at the presidential level, the conditional approach seemed to work. But in 1988, the dams broke. In addition to the $40 million from the public treasury, both the Republican and Democratic campaigns raised and spent other large sums on their campaigns. Informed observers estimate that such expenditures, made in addition to the money from the federal treasury, amounted to over $25 million for each party.

Attempts to stop such spending are exercises in futility. Whenever campaigns find it advantageous to spend money in excess of what is available from the government, or in excess of what the law allows, they will find a way to do so.

You Decide

☐ Should taxpayers' money be used to support political campaigns? Has experience at the presidential level been encouraging to the notion that publicly funded campaigns are less corrupt? Can we encourage cleaner, better, more competitive campaigns by giving cash to candidates and political parties?

☐ Can we adopt public financing of campaigns without hurting the chances of independent and third-party candidates? Is it a good idea to reinforce the two-party system in this way?

ABOLISHING THE ELECTORAL COLLEGE

The Existing Situation

In accordance with the Twelfth Amendment (which modifies the original language in Article II), the president and vice-president are chosen by electors. Those who serve as presidential electors do just one thing: they vote for their party's candidates for president and vice-president; they may not hold any other public office.

There are as many electors as there are members of Congress: Each state has one elector for each of its senators (that is, two per state) and one for each of its representatives in the House of Representatives (which are distributed among the states according to population). Thus, in 1988, tiny Delaware had three electors, and huge California had forty-seven.

In accordance with the Constitution, electors must cast their votes in their own states (usually their state capitals). The votes are sent to Washington and counted before a joint session of Congress. If any candidate gets the votes of a majority of electors, he or she becomes president. If no candidate gets a majority, the top three vote-getters are referred to the House of Representatives, where each state delegation gets one vote and a candidate must have the vote of a majority of the states to win.

As practices have evolved, states normally (by their own state laws) cast all of their electoral votes in a bloc. Thus, even if a candidate gains only 51 percent of the popular votes in a given state, he wins all of that state's electoral votes. (George Bush, for example, won 51 percent of the popular votes in California in 1988, but he got all 47 of its electoral votes.) That happens because each party presents a *slate* of candidates for elector. A plurality of votes for a given party's ticket enables its slate to win and become the state's electors.

Because states normally cast their electoral votes in blocs, it is possible (indeed, it happened, in 1888) that a candidate for president can win a plurality of the popular votes but lose in the electoral college. If a candidate wins close victories in states that command large blocs of electoral votes, he can beat an opponent who wins by large majorities in the rest of the states.

The vote of an elector is normally determined by the popular vote in a state, but not always. There have been a few cases (involving fewer than 20 individual electors) where electors have voted, not for the candidate to whom they were pledged, but for some other candidate. (The most recent example was a woman in West Virginia, who voted in 1988 for Senator Lloyd Bentsen for president, instead of Michael Dukakis, in order, she said, to draw attention to the absurdity of the electoral college. She later reportedly said she wished she had voted for Kitty Dukakis, which would apparently have been within her rights as an elector.) In a close election, the outcome could conceivably be in the hands of a small group of such "faithless electors." Some states have laws that seek to prevent an abandonment of electoral pledges, but these laws may not be enforceable, since the Constitution does not constrain electors, once chosen, in any way.

The Basic Proposal

RESOLVED: That the president be elected by a direct popular election.

ALTERNATIVE (addressed just to the problem of the "faithless elector"): That electors be eliminated and each state's electoral votes be cast automatically for the winner of a popular vote plurality in that state.

Discussion

The simplest way to do away with the electoral college would be to repeal the Twelfth Amendment and replace it with the direct popular election of the president.

If we did that, it might be desirable to require that a winning candidate receive not just a plurality of the popular votes, but a certain minimum percentage (say: 40 percent of the total votes cast). If no candidate won that percentage in the first round, there would be a run-off election between the top two finishers.

To prevent a candidate's winning the popular vote but losing the electoral college, an amendment might give a bloc of electoral votes (say: 100) to the winner of a popular-vote plurality nationwide. That would preserve the electoral college's emphasis on states in the presidential campaign, but make it virtually impossible for a candidate who lost the popular vote to win the presidency in the electoral college.

Relevant Facts

☐ It is impossible to tell from the cryptic reports of the debates at the Federal Convention of 1787 exactly why the framers established the system of electors. Some of them, no doubt, mistrusted the abilities of the people at large to make a suitable choice. George Mason, an old aristocrat from Virginia, spoke for this group when he said that expecting the people to choose a president would be like entrusting the choice of colors to a blind man. Unable to "see" the candidates properly, they would be unable to make discerning judgments.[25] Others, however, noting that governors in several of the states were chosen by the people directly, were ready to adopt the same method nationally. Gouverneur Morris, an influential young delegate from Pennsylvania, argued that, "If the people should elect, they will never fail to prefer some man of distinguished character, or services; some man . . . of continental reputation. If the legislature elects, it will be the work of intrigue, of cabal, of faction: it will be like the election of a pope by a conclave of cardinals. . . ."[26]

Ultimately, however, it was slavery that was decisive in preventing the framers from adopting a direct popular election of the president.[27]

Slaves of course did not vote, but southern states expected to be given weight in any scheme of representation for their slaves. In apportioning seats in the House of Representatives, for example, the Constitution counted five slaves as the equivalent of three free people. The electoral college was built on the distribution of seats in Congress, so southerners received additional weight in the choice of presidents because of their slaves, even though the slaves themselves could not vote. As Madison remarked at the Convention of 1787, "The substitution of electors [instead of a direct popular vote] obviated this difficulty [that is, slaves themselves not voting] and seemed on the whole to be liable to the fewest objections."[28] When the Thirteenth Amendment abolished slavery, this factor vanished—but by then, the electoral college was firmly established and apparently serving other purposes.

□ Concerning the suggested run-off if no candidate receives 40 percent of the vote: Has any president thus far in American history failed to achieve the 40 percent threshhold of popular votes? The answer is: yes. Abraham Lincoln won 39.6 percent of the popular vote in 1860, an election that included four major candidates. Lincoln's pluralities in 18 states translated into a decisive victory in the electoral college, where he got 180 votes, compared to 123 for his three opponents combined.

□ There have been a number of proposals through the years addressed to the problem of the "faithless elector." One is to abolish the office of elector and assign each state's vote automatically in proportion to a candidate's popular vote in the state.[29] An amendment to this effect gained the necessary two-thirds vote in the Senate in 1950, but failed in the House.

The House of Representatives has tended to favor plans that would substitute a direct popular election for the existing system. Proposals to this effect have been offered several times (in 1828, by President Andrew Jackson; in the 1870s, by Senator Charles Sumner of Massachusetts; and by a number of sponsors during the 1960s and 1970s). In 1963, the Supreme Court ruled that state legislative districts must conform to the principle of "one person, one vote."[30] The next year, the Court applied the same principle to congressional districting. This led the state of Delaware and twelve other states, in 1966, to petition the Supreme Court to outlaw the electoral college, on the ground that it denied people in small states a vote in the election of presidents equal to that of their fellow-citizens in large states,[31] but the Court refused to hear the case.

That same year (1966), Senator Birch Bayh (Democrat, Indiana), chair of the Senate Judiciary Subcommittee on Constitutional Amendments, announced his support for an amendment that would have abolished the electoral college and substituted a direct election plan. To discourage splinter parties, he said, Bayh proposed that a candidate would have to receive 40 percent of the popular vote to win; in the event that no candidate received enough to win in the first round, there would be a run-off between the top two candidates. In 1969, the House of Representatives voted 338-70 in favor of a direct-election amendment, but the best it ever did in the Senate, 51-49 in 1979, fell far short of the necessary two-thirds margin.

☐ By large majorities, respondents in public opinion polls have favored the direct election of presidents. The high-water mark was reached in 1981, when the Louis Harris organization found 77 percent in favor of a change to the direct election of the president; 21 percent were opposed.[32]

☐ The French president is chosen by direct popular vote. If no candidate receives over 50 percent of the vote in the first balloting, a run-off election is set between the top two vote-getters fourteen days later.

Arguments in Favor of This Proposal

1. Original Rationale. It is not clear why the framers established the electoral college. But whether it was because they lacked confidence in the political judgment of common people or to give weight to slave owners, we no longer share those beliefs. It is time to sweep away the obstacles and let the people choose the president directly. As journalist Neil Pierce wrote in 1981,

> Today the United States is approaching universal suffrage, so that every adult American, regardless of wealth, race or residence, will be able to vote and to have his vote counted equally and fairly. Suddenly, with the civil rights acts, . . . the death of the poll tax and the voting decisions of the courts, it is upon us. . . . It is the basic political fact of our times. And it is reflected in every American political institution—except the way we elect our president.[33]

There is no point trying to "fix" the electoral college by eliminating the electors or by requiring that the electors be chosen proportionally to the candidates' share of a given state's vote. The electoral college is the root of the problem. As Tom Wicker, columnist for the *New York Times,* has written, "The single reform that removes the inequities and perils of the present system without substituting others, that conforms to the long-range trend of American politics and society, is to eliminate the electoral college altogether and give the election of their president directly to the American people."[34]

2. Potential Danger. The electoral college is a dangerous, outmoded contraption which might bring the nation to a real crisis someday, by giving us a president for four years who had decisively lost the popular vote. Why wait until that happens before fixing it? It was one thing to have an "illegitimate" president at the end of the nineteenth century, when the national government had very little impact in the world and relatively little on the lives of ordinary citizens in this country. It would be quite a different matter under modern conditions.

3. Effect on Parties. The electoral college gives an unfair advantage to the two major parties. It stifles competition and muffles the expression of distinctive political opinions; it imposes a centrist conformity and leads to campaigns that offer a choice between two rich white men. We have made the nominating process more democratic by flushing the party bosses out of smoke-filled rooms and giving real importance to primaries, where grass-roots voters make their choices known. We need to carry that process to its logical conclusion, simplifying the presidential election itself and letting the people decide.

4. Vote Distribution. The distribution of votes in the electoral college is unfair. By the bloc-voting system, it gives too much weight to the larger states. And by the allocation of an elector for each senator, it gives too much weight to the smaller states. Michael Dukakis, the Democratic nominee in 1988, got 46 percent of the popular vote, but only 21 percent of the electoral vote. John Anderson in 1980 got 9 percent of the popular vote, but 0 percent of the electoral vote. Such distortions are unacceptable.

5. Effect on Voter Turnout. The electoral system discourages people from voting. Under the current system, because the winner-take-all system prevails in most states, a voter who lives in a state where one candidate appears to have a huge lead may decide that it is pointless to vote. If the outcome depended on the popular vote total nationwide, each vote in every state would count equally.

Arguments Against This Proposal

1. Original Rationale. The electoral college reflects the framers' belief that self-government is not a simple thing. Ours is a republic, not a simple democracy. We have a split legislature and a Supreme Court that can invalidate legislation that violates the Constitution. And we choose our presidents indirectly.

The party system has stripped some of the gears in the framers' design, reducing the independence of electors, but we ought not to tamper with it any further. The American people may not understand very well how the electoral college works, and they may sometimes be impatient with it, but there is no popular clamor to replace it. That is because the people basically support a system that provides a measure of indirection in self-government.

2. Potential Danger. Critics of the electoral college like to present an imaginary "parade of horribles." The fact is that the system works. It produces a decisive result quickly. It forestalls the quarrels about vote fraud that might arise if the outcome hung on a count of 100 million popular votes nationwide.

It is possible that a close election might produce a president whose legitimacy was questioned, but those or similar disturbances might come under any electoral system. Political leaders who contemplate a campaign for the presidency understand the existing rules, and the public would not listen for long to a candidate who lost by these rules and then complained about them. By the same token, a president who won the electoral college, even though he lost the popular vote, would have to proceed very cautiously in exercising the powers of his office.

3. Effect on Parties. The electoral college reinforces the two-party system. Because a candidate must win at least a plurality in a state in order to get any electoral votes at all, would-be splinter candidates are discouraged from mounting serious campaigns.

In countries like France, where there is a preliminary election for president and then a run-off, there are many candidates in the first round, and it is difficult for citizens to know how to cast their votes. Who among the favorites has the best chance to make it into the final election? Then, in the short period before the run-off election, political leaders maneuver and swap support. It is all very bewildering for the voters, and many are alienated by the process.

In a two-party system, the major parties work for many months formulating their platforms and deciding how to pitch their campaign. All of these efforts anticipate the November election, when the voters make their final choice. Thus, although a multi-party system seems to offer a wider range of choices, the voters have less control in the end. The two-party system ultimately offers voters the clearest choice and the greatest leverage over the people who prepare the choices.

4. Vote Distribution. The electoral college has been criticized for the way it distributes votes, but in fact, this method is ingenious. It gives the large states something (the potential to magnify their impact by casting their votes in a bloc), and it gives the small states something (more votes than their population alone would justify).

That is why the electoral college, despite its apparent deficiencies, has proven impervious to amendment. The large states would amend it one way (moving toward a direct popular election) and the small states another (eliminating the electors and directing states to split their electoral votes between the candidates according to the proportion each of them won). But reformers fail because they cannot get two-thirds of both houses of Congress, much less three-quarters of the states, to agree on any particular change.

5. Effect on Voter Turnout. Throwing the election into a vast, undifferentiated arena would almost certainly depress voting turnouts. In the 1988 presidential race, nearly 90 million votes were cast nationwide, making each individual's vote seem relatively insignificant. But by virtue of the electoral college, the contest was waged in statewide units, so campaign workers in a state such as New Jersey or Ohio could honestly hope to affect the outcome.

You Decide

☐ Does the electoral college violate the tenets of American democracy?

☐ How likely is it that the electoral college will seriously misfire?

☐ What effect would it have on the two-party system if we abolished the electoral college? Is that a serious consideration?

ELIMINATING THE VICE-PRESIDENCY

The Existing Situation

Article II of the Constitution provides for the election of a "Vice-President, chosen for the same term" as the president.

Originally the Constitution provided that the person who came in second for the presidency became vice-president, but since the ratification of the Twelfth Amendment in 1804, electors have cast "distinct" ballots for vice-president. Parties nominate a "ticket" for national offices, including separate candidates for president and vice-president.

As for succession in the event that a president is removed from office for impeachable offenses, or resigns, or dies, or is disabled during his term in office, Article II itself is silent. The Twenty-fifth Amendment, ratified in 1967, directs that, if a president is removed from office or dies or resigns, the vice-president shall become president. It further provides that, if the vice-president resigns or dies in office, the president shall nominate a successor, who takes office "upon confirmation by a majority vote of both houses of Congress." (This is, by the way, the only case where the House of Representatives votes on the confirmation of presidential appointments. In other cases, the Senate alone gives "advice and consent." The exception here was required to gain the House's approval for the amendment.)

Finally, the Twenty-fifth Amendment declares that, if the president is temporarily disabled, the vice-president assumes office as acting president. But if the president insists that he is fit to discharge his duties, "Congress shall decide the issue," by voting whether or not to support the finding of disability by the vice-president and a majority of the cabinet. To dislodge the president in the event of such disagreement requires a two-thirds vote in both houses of Congress.

The Basic Proposal

RESOLVED: That we should abolish the office of vice-president.

ALTERNATIVE: That the president, with confirmation by both houses of Congress, choose a vice-president after his inauguration.

Discussion

Either of these changes would require a constitutional amendment. An amendment to eliminate the vice-presidency would void all references to the office currently in the Constitution: most notably, the clause in Article II, Section 3, that makes the vice-president the presiding officer of the Senate, and the Twenty-fifth Amendment, which provides for vice-presidential succession in the event that a president can no longer serve.

The amendment would presumably direct that the Senate choose its own presiding officer (as the House now does). In addition, it would have to provide for succession. If a president were removed from office, or died, resigned, or became disabled, it might provide that Congress, by appropriate legislation, could designate someone to act as president until a new election filled the office.

If the elimination of the vice-presidency were deemed too radical, we might prefer to reform the selection process, as in the alternative above. Currently, the vice-president is elected with the president, on a ticket nominated by a political party. If the vice-president resigns or dies in office, the Twenty-fifth Amendment provides that the president, with the consent of Congress (majorities in both houses), appoints a successor.

A new constitutional amendment might direct that a president appoint a vice-president immediately after his own inauguration. Upon confirmation by *both* houses (different from the procedure for filling cabinet offices, but, like the Twenty-fifth Amendment, a provision that attracts support in the House of Representatives), the vice-president would assume office and take his or her place at the head of the line of succession to the presidency.

Relevant Facts

☐ In the course of American history, there have been three acts that governed succession to the presidency when a president for any reason leaves office. The first, passed by the Second Congress in 1792, assumed that the vice-president would "act" as president for the remainder of a president's term, and that if he too became unavailable, the president pro tempore of the Senate (traditionally the longest-serving senator) or, if there were none, the speaker of the House, would "act as president . . . until a president be elected." In the event of such a double vacancy, except during the last months of a presidential term, a special presidential election would be called the following November.

According to Edward Corwin, the framers of the Constitution assumed that the vice-president would remain vice-president and merely act as president, "and should become president only if and when he was elected as such."[35] Nevertheless, in 1841, when President William Henry Harrison died thirty-one days after his inauguration, John Tyler successfully asserted that he should not merely "act" as president for the balance of the term, but succeed to the office itself. Tyler's precedent governed in all subsequent instances of vice-presidential succession (by Millard Fillmore, Andrew Johnson, Chester Arthur, Theodore Roosevelt, Calvin Coolidge, Harry Truman, Lyndon Johnson, and Gerald Ford).

The succession act was changed in the 1880s. When President Garfield was assassinated in 1881, there happened to be neither a president pro tempore of the Senate nor a speaker of the House. If Chester Arthur had not been able to serve, the presidency would have been in limbo. Four years later, when Grover Cleveland's vice-president died in office, Republican control of the Senate put a leader of the opposition party next in line to the presidency, should anything have happened to Cleveland.

These circumstances led to a revision of the succession act. By the act of 1886, succession to the presidency went first to the vice-president, then down through the cabinet, beginning with the secretary of state, if he were constitutionally qualified, proceeding to the secretary of the treasury, and so on. This meant that control over the executive branch would normally not be transferred from one party to the other between elections.

The 1886 law preserved the principle of special elections. It provided that a cabinet officer act as president until the disability of the president or vice-president be removed or "a president shall be elected," and directed him to convene Congress within twenty days, presumably to provide for a special election.[36]

When Harry Truman succeeded to the presidency in 1945 (there was no vice-president, incidentally, for nearly four years), he expressed concern that, if he died or became disabled, the presidency would pass to an unelected official (the secretary of state). Even though Republicans controlled the House, and thus the speakership, in 1947 and 1948, Truman urged a return to the principles of the 1792 act, including the provision for special elections in the event that a leader of Congress had to "act" temporarily as president. In 1947, Congress enacted a new succession law (the one currently in force, subject since 1967 to the provisions of the Twenty-fifth Amendment), providing that the speaker of the House be next in line after the vice-president, but omitting any provision for a special election.

☐ There are many quotable remarks attesting to the insignificance of the vice-presidency. Most of them come from the period between the ratification of the Twelfth Amendment, which directed a distinct nomination for vice-presidential candidates (before that, John Adams and Thomas Jefferson had served in the office, and both succeeded to the presidency), and World War II, after which Truman's, Johnson's, and Ford's succession to the awesome responsibilities of the modern presidency dramatically underscored the importance of the office.

Besides John Nance Garner's famous remark that the vice-presidency was "not worth a pitcher of warm spit," there is the story of Boss Platt's delight in having conned Teddy Roosevelt into leaving New York State and accepting his party's nomination for the vice-presidency— an office that was "not a stepping stone to anything except oblivion," as Roosevelt himself observed. Asked whether he planned to attend McKinley's second inaugural, Platt cooed, "I am going to Washington to see Theodore take the veil."[37]

☐ The character of the vice-presidency and the quality of people nominated for the office have changed markedly since World War II. The office that was satirized in the 1932 Gershwin musical, "Of Thee I Sing," now lies just one heartbeat away from responsibility for our nuclear arsenal. The anguished public reaction to disclosures and rumors about the mental health of the initial Democratic nominee for vice-president in 1972 showed how carefully modern vice-presidential nominees would be scrutinized. The political stature of recent nominees is suggested by the fact that six of the eight most recent vice-presidents have subsequently won presidential nominations for themselves.[38] Michael Nelson notes that the five "successor presidents" in the twentieth century (Theodore Roosevelt, Coolidge, Truman, Johnson and Ford) have been rated by historians higher on average than the 11 elected presidents, and he argues that in recent years, vice-presidential nominees have often been better qualified than their presidential running mates (he cites John Sparkman in 1952, Estes Kefauver in 1956, Johnson and Henry Cabot Lodge in 1960, Walter Mondale in 1976, Bush in 1980 and Lloyd Bentsen in 1988).

□ The custom of permitting the presidential nominee to choose his vice-presidential running mate began in 1940, when FDR chose Henry Wallace. Prior to that time, those who chose the presidential nominee (the congressional caucus until 1824; party conventions after 1832) decided on his running mate as well.

□ For 38 of its 201 years (through 1988), the nation has been without a vice-president.

□ In the 185 years since the ratification of the Twelfth Amendment, only two vice-presidents—Martin Van Buren and George Bush—advanced directly to the presidency by election. Others won the nomination of their parties (John C. Breckinridge in 1861, Hubert Humphrey in 1968, Walter Mondale in 1984), but failed in the general election.

□ Between the resignation of Nixon in August, 1974, and the inauguration of Carter in January, 1977, the United States for the first time in its history had both a president (Ford) and vice-president (Nelson Rockefeller, after his confirmation according to the Twenty-fifth Amendment in December, 1974) who had gained office not through election, but by appointment. No one outside Ford's congressional district in Michigan had ever voted for either man for an office in the national government.

□ Only a few modern constitutions have vice-presidents who succeed to the presidency in the event of presidential death or disability. Most provide for a special election. In France, for example, an election must be held within thirty-five days to replace the president; in the meantime, the president of the Senate acts as president. If the president of Israel dies in office, a new president is elected within thirty days.

Arguments in Favor of This Proposal

1. Importance of Election. The office of vice-president is a constitutional afterthought. The position was contrived by the framers solely to ensure that presidential electors would vote for at least one candidate outside their own state. With the passage of the Twelfth Amendment, even that reason evaporated. As the 1792 Succession Act makes clear, the founding generation believed that "no one who had not been elected to the presidency should serve as president any longer than necessary to organize a new presidential election."[39] Let no one be president unless he or she is elected to the position. If a president dies in office or cannot continue to serve, let us elect a successor, with a caretaker serving until a new election can be arranged.

2. Qualifications. The process for selecting vice-presidential candidates is scandalously haphazard. A presidential candidate who has devoted all his energies to his own race must decide on a running mate in the frenzy of final preparations for his own nomination and acceptance speech, and his choice is automatically ratified by a convention that would not think of embarrassing him as he embarks on the general campaign. As a result, the person nominated gets far less searching scrutiny than a president's later choices for cabinet offices or the Supreme Court.

No one outside the candidates' immediate circle of advisers had an opportunity to examine and comment on the fitness for the presidency of Spiro Agnew, Thomas Eagleton, Geraldine Ferraro, or J. Danforth Quayle. The present system is a lottery, and we have had too many losers.

3. Selection Criteria. Even a presidential candidate who takes his responsibility in choosing a vice-presidential running mate quite seriously has other things in mind besides fitness for the presidency. He must think about his own compatibility with the person and about balancing the ticket; these considerations do not necessarily point to a person fit to be president, much less one who could be elected on his or her own merits to national office.

4. Usefulness of Position. The job itself is without substance. Its sole constitutional duty—presiding over the Senate—is in fact legislative. Actually, vice presidents rarely preside in person over the Senate, except when a close vote is anticipated and their casting vote may be needed to break a tie.

Arguments Against This Proposal

1. Importance of Election. By the framers' own design—both in its original form and by the Twelfth Amendment—the vice-president is elected by a national constituency. Voters understand perfectly well that they are choosing a ticket and that if anything happens to the president, the vice-president takes over.

2. Qualifications. Certainly there have been vice-presidents, and vice-presidential candidates, who seem unqualified to many observers. The same can be said of some presidents. In fact, the way a candidate handles the selection of a running mate offers a good test of his or her fitness for the presidency. The electorate's assessment of this decision probably has some effect on the candidate's success in November. A candidate who consults too narrowly or chooses badly deserves to suffer.

3. Selection Criteria. Most recent vice-presidential nominees have in fact been remarkably well qualified for the presidency. That is no accident. Presidential nominees generally seek running mates who are experienced and well known and who will wear well through the rigors of a national campaign. Recent embarrassments are the exceptions that will reinforce this rule.

4. Usefulness of Position. As the responsibilities of the presidency have grown, so have those of the vice-presidency. Vice President Mondale was a major player in the Carter administration, and it is no exaggeration to say that he got valuable on-the-job training for the presidency which would have served him, if he had ever had to assume that office. The same thing was true when Bush served as vice-president in the Reagan administration. Everyone, including the president, knows that the vice-president may succeed to the presidency at any moment. That is why vice-presidents, at least since Lyndon Johnson in 1961, have been given offices in the building next to the White House.[40]

You Decide

☐ Does our system of government need a vice-president?

☐ Should anyone succeed to the presidency without having won a national election? If not, is it sufficient to have run in second place?

☐ Should the Constitution, by amendment, reform the method for selecting vice-presidents?

8
How Government Works Together

ALLOWING MEMBERS OF CONGRESS TO SERVE IN THE ADMINISTRATION

The Existing Situation

Article I, Section 6, of the Constitution (the so-called "incompatibility clause") keeps the two branches strictly separated. It bars a member of the House or Senate from accepting an appointment to the president's cabinet or to any office in the executive branch without first resigning his or her seat in Congress.

The Basic Proposal

RESOLVED: That members of Congress should be eligible to serve in the president's cabinet without having to give up their seats in Congress.

Discussion

To achieve this purpose, we would need an amendment repealing the "incompatibility clause." In addition, the amendment could *require* the president, or authorize Congress by law, to designate that certain positions, or a certain number of positions (15? 50?), be reserved for members of Congress.

Relevant Facts

☐ Most of the framers of the Constitution believed that there should be strict separation between Congress and the executive branch. George Mason of Virginia said, "I consider this clause [the one that prevented the president from appointing members of Congress to high administrative office] as the corner-stone on which our liberties depend. . . ." He hoped we could avoid "the abuses and corruption in the British Parliament," where the crown bent the will of elected representatives by dangling out the hope of appointment to lucrative office.

A few of the framers disagreed. Nathaniel Gorham of Massachusetts went so far as to contend that "this corruption [in Britain] has its advantage, as it gives stability to their government."[1] Alexander Hamilton was of the same opinion. But support for the prohibition was widespread at the 1787 Convention.

□ The constitutions of other modern democracies present a range of alternatives on this point. In Great Britain, the prime minister and the members of her cabinet, who head the major departments of government, are members of Parliament. In fact they become cabinet members by virtue of being leaders of the dominant party in Parliament. In West Germany, the chancellor and ministers need not be, but usually are, members of the lower house of the parliament (the Bundestag). In France, the premier and ministers may not hold seats in parliament, though in practice most are chosen from parliament and resign their seats in favor of an alternate who was elected with them.

□ The doctrine of strict separation has not been consistently followed in American practice. George Washington, for example, in 1794 appointed the sitting chief justice of the Supreme Court, John Jay, to negotiate a vital treaty with Great Britain. Many today would oppose such an appointment on the grounds that a Supreme Court justice, considering a case involving a treaty, ought not to be compromised by having been a party to its framing and ratification. Even so, modern justices (Felix Frankfurter, Abe Fortas) have occasionally served as informal advisers to presidents.

The separation between the executive and the legislature is also sometimes breached. In recent times, members of Congress have served with administrators on task forces to develop reforms of the social security program. Such bodies apparently do not violate the "incompatibility clause," because members of Congress are not assuming direction of any administrative function. Nevertheless, they do represent a blurring of the distinction between the legislative and executive branches as delineated in the Constitution.

Arguments in Favor of This Proposal

1. Deadlock. Too often, the president and Congress are at one another's throats. Instead of cooperating in the search for good policies, they stand fast behind their own positions and point at the other body as the one responsible for the nation's troubles.

On the budget deficit, for example, Congress defended the principal items of domestic spending, while President Reagan insisted that we must increase defense spending and reduce taxes. Everyone agreed that the resulting deficits were eroding the foundations of our economy, and many officials in both branches had a plan for balancing the budget, but the deadlock continued because the political incentives in the system favor confrontation, rather than compromise and a cooperative search for better policies.

2. Effect on Bureaucracy. In America, bureaucracies have the reputation of being alien, of imposing regulations from afar and of being tangled up in red tape. Politicians, capitalizing on this feeling, often run "against Washington," promising to get the government off our backs.

If members of Congress headed the bureaucracies, they might seem less remote and less "pointy-headed," to borrow a term from George Wallace. (Wallace, former governor of Alabama, was a candidate for the presidency in 1968 and 1972.) Henry Reuss puts the point more graciously when he remarks that members of Congress would bring a "hometown touch" to the agencies of government.

3. Recruitment for Government Service. Appointive government service is not a valued profession in this country. In France and Japan, the ablest graduates of the leading colleges often aspire to a career of government service; in America, that is far less often the case. This amendment would help to attract better people to political careers, with the prospect of a place in the cabinet for those who achieved distinction in Congress. And it would give a president many more capable people to choose from when he puts together his cabinet.

There are many reasons for this tendency to disparage the work of government and those who do it. But if a presidential appointment to a high administrative position came to be seen as a fit reward for distinguished congressional service, it might help to overcome this prejudice and draw the ablest talents to public service, both legislative and administrative.

4. Could One Person Handle Both Jobs? Most of the detail work in both branches is done by aides. Jack Kemp, secretary of housing and urban development, does not oversee particular building projects; he sets policy and oversees the work of agency heads. Similarly, Senator Barbara Mikulski of Maryland cannot by herself do all of the things that we associate with being a senator. She has a large staff, who open and sort and prepare answers for her mail, who greet her constituents in Maryland and when they visit Washington, and who set up her work on legislative committees (arranging hearings, identifying the leading issues, briefing the senator, drafting committee reports and legislation).

Recognizing this staff assistance does not mean that we minimize the secretary's or the senator's personal contribution. They are responsible for the outcomes, and they contribute specifically by appointing aides and supervising their work. Above all they set the tone— more or less, depending on their strength and clarity of purpose. This, too, is the essential contribution that one person would make if he or she held leading positions in both branches at the same time. The key function would be to help *fuse* the outlook and purposes of the two branches.

5. Conflicts of Interest. It cannot be denied that a cabinet secretary who also represented a district in Congress would be in a position to favor that district in administrative decisions, but that is little different from a representative or senator who chairs a powerful committee in Congress. It is well known that the renaissance of Charleston, South Carolina, owes much to the attentions of Congressman W. Mendel Rivers, who represented that city in Congress and for many years chaired the House Armed Services Committee. Rivers could not have done any more for Charleston had he been secretary of defense. On the other hand, his favoritism might have been more closely watched by the press.

6. Tension Between House and Senate. Again, it cannot be denied that one chamber (the Senate, for example) may be miffed if the president appoints a cabinet secretary from the other (the House). Political choice always entails bruised feelings. Probably some customary ways of distributing these honors would develop to lessen the collision of big egos. They might, for example, be alternated.

7. Disrupted Balances. It is difficult to predict which side, Congress or the president, would be strengthened if this proposal were adopted. The desire for presidential appointments might soften opposition in Congress. On the other hand, the expectation that certain members of Congress were entitled to appointment might limit a president's options, but the system's checks and balances would still work. The president could still veto legislation if he wanted to. And if evidence began to accumulate that the president were abusing his powers, Congress would have the leverage to bring him to account.

Congress' great and unique strength among the world's legislatures might be diminished somewhat—that is the price we may have to pay to counter the tendency to stalemate. But Congress would remain a formidable force, with independent political roots in the electorate.

8. *Campaign Advantages.* A member of Congress who chairs a powerful committee already has substantial advantages when campaigning for reelection. Making her a member of the cabinet may increase her power somewhat, but it also heightens her responsibility and exposure. It is a price we should pay for increased coherence and responsibility.

Arguments Against This Proposal

1. *Deadlock.* The Constitution enables the electorate to choose the person it wants to be chief executive, and each district and state to choose legislators according to its desires for those offices. If the branches conflict on policy, it is usually because the people are themselves in conflict. The government ought not to act decisively when the people are still uncertain. The framers created a system biased against radical changes in policy. If a truly serious situation develops and the people become determined to act (as in 1861 and 1932 and 1964), the system is not incapable of moving decisively.

2. *Effect on Bureaucracy.* Candidates who run "against Washington" are appealing to something deep in American culture. Our Revolutionary tradition pitted the love of liberty against the lust for power; the separation of powers was designed in part to protect liberty against power. The strength of Congress and its independence from the bureaucracy is indeed a bulwark of liberty.

3. *Recruitment for Government Service.* It would not improve the standing of bureaucracy in American culture to have it headed by members of Congress. The animus against government is rooted in anti-elitism, suspicions about rationality and a jealous attitude toward power, especially remote power.[2] These attitudes are part of the spirit that would resist this proposal, and they would persist even if the proposal were somehow adopted. The nations that have a high tradition of government service (Britain, France, Japan) are nations with an aristocratic tradition. That is not a coincidence. We do not have such a tradition, and we should not try to imitate the countries that do.

As for recruitment of able candidates, there is no lack of desire among people with an instinct for public service for serving in Congress. And presidents have little difficulty finding capable people to join the cabinet. In fact, many members of Congress have been willing to give up their seats to do so. Besides, in a nation of 250 million people, it does not diminish the pool much to eliminate 535 prospects.

4. Could One Person Handle Both Jobs? Experienced people insist that it is not possible for one person to do a good job at being both a cabinet officer and a member of Congress. Running one of the major departments of government takes all the time and energy a person has to give. Should he or she have to miss many votes in Congress, the result would be poor performance in both jobs. The system works in parliamentary regimes only because of the presence of senior, career civil servants. Our civil service does not attain this level.

There are similar problems on the other side. The work of representing a congressional district or a state is very demanding, and it ought not to be delegated any further than is necessary. In other traditions, the tie between a representative and his or her constituents is not nearly as close as it is in the U.S. Here a person who aspires to represent a district must ordinarily have lived there for many years and know its people intimately. Constituents need to be able to trust their representative to stand up for their interests instinctively and without conflicting loyalties.

5. Conflicts of Interest. An interior secretary from Montana who represented mining interests in Congress or a commerce secretary from Connecticut who represented a large electronics business could not help but favor those to whom he owed his seat in Congress. The separation of administration from representation is a wise arrangement.

6. Tension Between House and Senate. Legislative power in most parliamentary systems centers on a single chamber. Thus, when the cabinet includes the leading members of the house of commons (or deputies), there can be a true fusion of executive and legislative powers, if that is desired. In our system, legislative power is divided between two chambers, each of which jealously guards its prerogatives. Thus, if the chair of the House Armed Services Committee became secretary of defense, his Senate counterpart might be particularly alert to weaknesses in the administration's program. This tendency would be even worse if the two chambers happened to be controlled by different parties (as was the case between 1981 and 1987). The American system is simply not designed for a fusion of powers. We cannot have the advantages of the parliamentary system while retaining the basic architecture of our system of separated powers. They are two different approaches to the design and operation of constitutional democracy. It is a mistake to try to blend them.

7. Disrupted Balances. Our system is one of balance, and this proposal would disturb that balance. It might give the president too much control, by allowing him to dangle appointments in front of leading members of Congress and then coopting those leaders once they had become part of the administration. Or it might weaken the president, by forcing him to come to terms with the leading barons of Congress, rather than staking out an independent course and seeking to bring the pressure of public opinion on Congress to adopt it, in the manner of an Andrew Jackson or Ronald Reagan. In either case, it would disrupt the countervailance which permits vigorous executive leadership (in the manner of Lincoln and the Roosevelts), but also enables Congress to thwart a president (like Nixon) who is deemed to have abused his powers.

8. Campaign Advantages. Members of Congress who were also cabinet secretaries would normally have a tremendous advantage in campaigning for reelection. Imagine a senator, two years into her service as secretary for housing and urban affairs, running for reelection as senator from Maryland. Or a member of the House, as secretary of defense, running for reelection in a district with huge defense facilities. Our system depends on separating lawmaking from administrative decision-making (appointments, making contracts). This proposal strikes at the root of that fundamental principle.

You Decide

☐ Can one person handle both jobs: representing a constituency in Congress and heading a major administrative department?

☐ Would it weaken the executive power if the president were expected to appoint legislative leaders to his administration?

☐ How would Congress be affected as an independent legislative body if it became a forum for the administration? Would the standing of individual members who were also members of the administration diminish?

☐ Is there too much confrontation between the branches under the Constitution? Would it be wise to encourage greater cooperation?

ENCOURAGING DIRECT PRESIDENTIAL DIALOGUE WITH CONGRESS

The Existing Situation

Article II of the Constitution states that the president "shall from time to time give to the Congress information on the state of the union." This clause provides the basis for the president's annual State of the Union address, traditionally presented in January. In addition, in times of crisis or when major issues arise, modern presidents[3] occasionally speak to the nation before joint sessions of Congress. Also, cabinet officers and other leading officials of the executive branch appear regularly before congressional committees to explain administration policies and answer questions.

The Basic Proposal

RESOLVED: That the president ought to appear regularly before major congressional committees to present the policies of his administration and to answer questions.

ALTERNATIVE: That cabinet officers ought to be made ex-officio, non-voting members of both houses of Congress, so that they could present the administration's legislative program and answer questions about their own performance.

Discussion

It would not require a constitutional amendment to achieve the purpose of the basic proposal outlined here. Presidential appearances before congressional committees could happen if both sides were able to agree on a mutually acceptable set of arrangements.

The approach in the alternative resolution would probably require a constitutional amendment. It would modify the separation of powers by introducing cabinet officers into Congress, but without a vote. Denying them the vote is necessary in order to preserve the representational pattern in the Constitution, protected especially by the clause in Article V that guarantees that "no state, without its consent, shall be deprived of its equal suffrage in the Senate." Instead of putting members of Congress in the president's cabinet (as in the previous proposal), this amendment would seek to bridge the separation of powers from the other end, by putting cabinet members in Congress.

Relevant Facts

☐ There is only one well-documented instance of a sitting president appearing before a congressional committee to answer questions. On October 17, 1974, President Ford appeared before the House Judiciary Committee's Subcommittee on Criminal Justice to present a prepared statement and answer questions about his pardon of former President Nixon. The purpose of his visit was to respond to contentions that Nixon had yielded the presidency in return for a promise that he would not have to face criminal prosecution. Ford insisted, "I want to assure you, members of this subcommittee, members of Congress and the American people, there was no deal, period. . . ."

Earlier, when the subcommittee requested information about the pardon, Ford had submitted a short cover letter and copies of a televised speech and press-conference answers to questions about the pardon. House members characterized this response as "unsatisfactory, cavalier, and very close to being disrespectful to the House of Representatives." Subcommittee member Bella Abzug (Democrat, New York) commented, "I don't believe press releases thrown out to the public are serious answers."

When Ford made his dramatic appearance before the subcommittee, he made it clear that he had come voluntarily, and he insisted that his visit set no precedent. The White House cited two earlier appearances by presidents before House committees, one by Washington and another by Lincoln, but neither is well documented. Two other presidents, John Tyler and Theodore Roosevelt, testified before congressional committees, but only after their terms in office had expired.[4]

□ All twentieth-century presidents have held press conferences, but practices have varied widely. For Theodore Roosevelt, they were more in the form of lectures than question-and-answer sessions. Wilson in his first term met frequently with reporters, but in his second term he tended to prefer formal addresses to Congress and public speaking tours. Harding and Coolidge required written questions in advance.

FDR was the champion of dialogue with reporters. He normally held two short sessions each week throughout his three-plus terms, 992 in all. Truman and Eisenhower cut back on the number of press conferences, but Eisenhower permitted television to use clips on delayed rebroadcast. Kennedy was the first to permit live television, of which he made adroit use. Johnson and Nixon were far less comfortable with the electronic media; as their administrations became mired in controversy, their sessions with the press became less frequent and were sometimes marked by antagonistic exchanges. Ford and Carter met the press regularly, but not frequently. In eight years, Reagan held forty-eight press conferences. As with many of his predecessors, the numbers diminished as his tenure wore on and he tended to favor other, less spontaneous forms of communication with the public.

□ Joseph Story, a Supreme Court justice and author of the influential *Commentaries of the Constitution,* first published in 1833, lent his authority to the argument in favor of giving cabinet members a seat in Congress without a vote. Concerned that the executive was working its influence silently and secretly, Story believed that putting cabinet officers in Congress would be a step in the direction of greater accountability.[5]

During the Civil War, George Pendleton, a Democratic member of the House from Ohio, presented a bill to authorize cabinet members to participate in congressional debates on matters affecting their departments and to require them, twice weekly, to be present in Congress for questioning. A select committee chaired by Pendleton reported his bill with approval, saying that it would cause the administration's influence in Congress to be "open, declared, and authorized, rather than secret, concealed, and unauthorized," but the bill died when the House adjourned before taking a vote on it. In 1881, Pendleton, by then a senator, offered a similar bill. It too was endorsed by a select committee, but never came to a vote. Opponents challenged the constitutionality of Pendleton's measure, but supporters argued that the Constitution prevented only voting rights for non-elected members, leaving Congress free to admit anyone to participate in its debates.[6]

Woodrow Wilson, as a young political scientist, argued for "responsible cabinet government" in the United States. Its principal features would have been to give the heads of the executive departments— the members of the cabinet—seats in Congress, with the privilege of initiating legislation, and to require a cabinet officer to resign if he failed to gain passage for legislation in his jurisdiction; he would have required the president and whole cabinet to resign if the administration sustained major defeats in Congress. The adoption of Wilson's idea would have brought us close to the parliamentary form of government. In Wilson's eyes, the great virtue of such a system was that it would promote lively and pertinent debate, which was "the best, the only effective, means of educating public opinion," and thus encourage effective and accountable government.[7]

In the early twentieth century, President Taft proposed the idea of a unified national budget and, in a special message to Congress, suggested that cabinet members be given non-voting seats in Congress so that they could present and defend the president's budget in congressional debate. Wilson succeeded Taft as president, but by that time, he was convinced that strong presidential leadership, in informal collaboration with his party's leaders in Congress, could develop enough unity and discipline to make the existing system effective.[8]

Hedrick Smith, formerly Washington bureau chief of *The New York Times,* has recently renewed the idea that leading members of the administration, including the president, ought to appear periodically before Congress to answer questions. Smith argues that press conferences are a poor substitute for the close questioning of government officials that occurs in parliamentary systems.[9]

Arguments in Favor of This Proposal

(N.B.: Many of the arguments in the previous section, concerning the proposal to allow members of Congress to serve in the executive branch, are pertinent here. See especially the pro and con arguments numbered 1, 5, and 8. In this section, we confine ourselves to arguments about the value of bringing the administration into a more regular, direct dialogue with Congress.)

1. Presidential Leadership. As the record on press conferences shows, presidents who are politically besieged sometimes go into hiding. In addition, presidents who are ill, or their handlers (as in the case of President Wilson after his stroke in October, 1919[10]), can mask their disability by simply refusing to go into public. We need a mechanism that obliges the president to demonstrate that he is in control and can defend his policies.

2. Voluntary Arrangements. The press conference is no substitute for the kind of questioning that takes place between peers in a parliamentary system. Reporters present tough questions, but they are not represen-tatives of the public in any satisfactory sense. If they confront a president too directly, they arouse resentment and run the risk of compromising their role of impartiality. The presidency is a position of political leadership. The person who holds that position ought to face his or her political peers. The dialogue will always be unequal, owing to the president's position as chief executive and chief of state, but in his political aspect, he ought to be made directly answerable to the political opposition.

3. Shared Purpose. As for the alternative proposal: If the leading members of the administration were regularly on the floor of Congress, a greater sense of shared purpose and political stakes between the branches would be encouraged. The administrators serving in Congress could explain and defend the president's positions. Anticipating that they would have to defend them in Congress, they would work on the executive side for policies that would be viewed favorably in Congress. The nation would benefit from the increased incentives to cooperation and the lessening of the system's inclination toward confrontation.

4. Influence on the Quality of Debate. Either of these proposals would elevate the level of public debate about political issues. Ours is a system of self-government. If it is going to work, the people must be educated. Attending to a debate and dialogue directly among our leaders would promote that education—particularly if the debate occurred with the immediate prospect of decision about important questions, and even resignation, as Woodrow Wilson proposed. A further consequence might be that there would be a premium, in the selection of presidents and cabinet officers, on an ability to present and defend policies forcefully and effectively.

Arguments Against This Proposal

1. Presidential Leadership. If the president or cabinet secretaries have something to tell Congress, they already have many ways to communicate; and if Congress wants to call the administration on the carpet, it has plenty of ways to do that, too. It is not necessary, or wise, to formalize these relationships any further.

As for cases of serious presidential disability, there are other ways of solving that problem without compromising the doctrine of the separation of powers. See the Twenty-fifth Amendment.

2. Voluntary Arrangements. Under the American constitutional system, the president is co-equal with Congress. It would pervert the framers' design to make the president answerable to Congress. He is not subject to subpoena by the courts, and he ought not to be hauled before Congress, much less congressional committees, against his will. As for voluntary arrangements, he should be wary of setting any precedents and resist any formula for regular appearances. Congress and the courts have many ways to bring the administration to account. It would disturb the system's carefully constructed balances to modify them in the way contemplated in this proposal.

3. Shared Purpose. As for the alternative proposal: Congress and the administration feel a sense of shared purpose when they both reflect the people's will. Otherwise, they ought not to. The proposal blurs the line between legislative and executive responsibility, without adding anything useful to the dialogue that currently exists between the branches in such forums as congressional committee hearings.

4. Influence on the Quality of Debate. Wilson's model was the parliamentary system. Whether the debate that occurs in parliament does or does not promote public education, it depends on a totally different format of constitutional powers. Our system achieves public participation by different means: lobbying, demonstrating, letter-writing campaigns, testimony before congressional hearings—and all of it broadcast over television. Our leaders may be less engaging debaters than those in parliamentary countries, but a debating society is not the only model for effective democratic government.

You Decide

☐ Would it be valuable if the president were required regularly to stand up and face questions directly from Congress?

☐ What effect would it have on the prestige of Congress as an independent legislative body if it became a forum for the administration, as contemplated in the alternative proposal?

☐ Is there any merit to Woodrow Wilson's idea that a president whose administration repeatedly faces defeat in Congress ought to resign?

PUTTING NEW CONTROLS ON WAR POWERS

The Existing Situation

The Constitution divides the "war powers" (originally Lincoln's term, meaning control over the use of military force) between the president and Congress. Before the nation can apply military force, Congress must have exercised its power to "raise and support armies" and "provide and maintain a navy."[11] The president as commander in chief of the armed forces must be willing to send those troops into situations where conflict may develop. In addition, the Constitution gives Congress power to "declare war," though it does not define "war."

In 1973, Congress passed the War Powers Resolution (WPR), over President Nixon's veto. Representing itself as a clarification of the Constitution's intent, the resolution requires the president to "consult" with "Congress" (without defining either of those terms), in every practicable case, before sending military forces into potentially hostile situations. It calls on him to report to Congress within 48 hours after he has committed armed forces to hostile situations. And it requires a congressional resolution of support if the troops are to be used for an extended period. If Congress refuses to pass such a resolution, the WPR states that the president must withdraw the forces within sixty days. He may use an additional thirty days to effect an orderly withdrawal.

(More details about the background, provisions, and criticisms that have been made of the WPR can be found toward the end of Chapter 4, above.)

The Basic Proposal

RESOLVED: That we need a process for involving the president and congressional leaders *together* in making decisions that lead to the use of military force.

Discussion

To implement this proposal, a president might offer to meet with a core group of congressional leaders at least once each month and review situations around the world that were raising concerns about national security and might require the use of American military force. The core group might include the speaker and minority leader of the House, the majority and minority leaders of the Senate, the chair and ranking minority member of the Senate Foreign Relations Committee, the House Foreign Affairs Committee, and the House and Senate Armed Services and Intelligence Committees. If the president reported to the congressional leaders that he had committed military forces to a potentially hostile situation, or if he told them of his intention to do so, they might oblige themselves to prepare a resolution of support or opposition for the action and obtain a congressional vote within a certain number of days. Or, if the congressional leaders on their own found that the president had introduced armed forces into a potentially hostile situation, they might likewise submit a resolution of approval or disapproval for expeditious congressional consideration. (This version is modeled on a proposal by Senators Robert Byrd [Democrat, West Virginia], the majority leader, and Sam Nunn [Democrat, Georgia], chairman of the Armed Services Committee, prepared for consideration by the Senate in 1988. The Byrd-Nunn proposal would have been based on a statute, rather than the initiative of the president in establishing these regular consultations.)

An alternative way to induce the president to share his war powers would be to amend the act passed in 1947 that created the National Security Council (NSC). As revised in 1949, the Council has six statutory members: the president and vice-president, the secretaries of state and defense, the chairman of the Joint Chiefs of Staff (the senior military officer), and the director of the Central Intelligence Agency (CIA). The statutory function of the Council is to advise the president with respect to the integration of domestic, foreign and military policies relating to national security. Inasmuch as the principal function of the Council is to advise the president, he is of course free to invite whomever else he chooses to attend its meetings. The Council also has a staff, headed by the national security adviser (General Brent Scowcroft, for President Bush). The NSC plays a crucial role as a gatherer of background information for presidential consideration and as an expediter of his decisions. The person who heads the NSC staff is one of the key figures in the government.

To introduce members of Congress into the administration's councils without compromising the president's ultimate responsibility in this area, a new amendment to the 1949 act might provide that the president choose four members of Congress to serve on the NSC: two from each chamber and two from each party. Like everyone else on the NSC, these congressional members would serve on the Council (though not, of course, in Congress) at the president's pleasure; that is, they would be subject to his removal and replacement. They would be entitled to sit with the NSC whenever it met and allowed to review all documents and papers in the Council staff's keeping, with the understanding that they must respect the secrecy of these materials.

Relevant Facts

☐ Through the first two centuries of constitutional government, there were many situations short of declared war in which the nation employed military force.[12] In each of these cases, the president made the decision to use military force. Until about 1950, however, presidents were careful to discuss their plans with leading members of Congress before acting, and none ever claimed any inherent power to wage war on his own authority.[13]

Since the mid-twentieth century, that pattern has changed. Presidents have occasionally sent troops into battle without consulting Congress at all, or with only a perfunctory, tardy, and sometimes misleading effort at informing certain sympathetic members of their plans. Such was the case for Korea (with President Truman) and Indochina (Presidents Kennedy, Johnson and Nixon), and for Grenada and Libya (President Reagan).

☐ Every president since Nixon (who vetoed the resolution) has insisted that the WPR is unconstitutional and unwise. They argue that it attempts to restrict the exercise of powers given to the president, not by legislation, but by the Constitution; and that it invites our adversaries to thwart American security interests simply by hanging on for sixty days. Under the existing resolution, unless Congress takes positive action, the president must withdraw the troops. Presidents from Ford and Carter through Reagan have argued that it is unreasonable to expect Congress, in sixty days, to resolve its doubts and endorse a venture that may be full of risks.

Many members of Congress admit the force of these objections, but insist that the spirit of our constitutional system is violated when one person, assisted by others who serve at his pleasure, can take the nation to war.

☐ In *The Federalist,* number 23, Alexander Hamilton states the case for granting "powers . . . without limitation" in the field of national defense. "The circumstances that endanger the safety of nations are infinite, and for this reason no constitutional shackles can wisely be imposed on the power to which the care of it is committed." Hamilton's argument is sometimes misunderstood. The context makes clear that Hamilton is calling for unbounded national (not specifically presidential) authority in the field of national defense, overriding the claims of the states. Later (in *The Federalist,* number 75), defending the arrangement that made the president share the treaty-making power with the Senate, Hamilton writes, "The history of human conduct does not warrant that exalted opinion of human virtue which would make it wise in a nation to commit interests of so delicate and momentous a kind, as those which concern its intercourse with the rest of the world, to the sole disposal of a magistrate created and circumstanced as would be a President of the United States."[14]

☐ Abraham Lincoln, then a representative in Congress, in a letter in 1848 to his law partner, W. H. Herndon, criticized President Polk's actions in taking the United States into the Mexican War. He wrote, "The provision of the Constitution giving the war-making power to Congress was dictated, as I understand it, by the following reasons. Kings had always been involving and impoverishing their people in wars, pretending generally, if not always, that the good of the people was the object. This our Convention understood to be the most oppressive of all kingly oppressions, and they resolved to so frame the Constitution that *no one man* should hold the power of bringing this oppression upon us."[15]

☐ The Supreme Court has so far been unwilling to enforce the WPR.[16] At the time of the naval operation in the Persian Gulf, several members of Congress, led by Mike Lowry (Democrat, Washington), brought suit, asking the courts to find that President Reagan had introduced armed forces into a potentially hostile situation and was therefore obliged to report to Congress and set the 60-day "clock" ticking. The Court refused, taking the position that the dispute was not ripe for adjudication. Congress had not yet exhausted its powers to curb presidential action, if indeed it was the will of a majority of Congress to do so. The Court further suggested that the case might have been different if Congress as a whole had resolved that the circumstances in the Gulf warranted the application of the WPR. In fact, Congress was unable to pass such a resolution, and the suit had been brought by just a handful of its Members.[17]

The decision in this case was similar to many others of recent vintage in the field of war powers. In 1982, for example, twenty-nine members of the House charged that President Reagan had violated the

WPR by sending military personnel to El Salvador without the required consultation or report. In response, sixteen senators and thirteen representatives asked the Court *not* to intervene in this political dispute but to leave it to the regular legislative process. The Court decided that it would not be appropriate for a judicial body to undertake the fact-finding that would be necessary to settle this dispute.[18]

Arguments in Favor of This Proposal

1. Judging the Resolution. The WPR represents the right ideal: requiring that the president and Congress join in determining the need to send men and women into battle. But even its strongest supporters agree that the WPR has not worked very well. Presidents have only sporadically and reluctantly abided by the reporting requirement, and they have sometimes openly refused to consult before sending armed forces into battle. And a president cannot be coerced.

If the WPR is ever going to work, it must be amended. If Congress is ever going to play a positive role in foreign affairs, it must specify which leaders are authorized to act in the consultative process, and it must agree to vote, up or down, on a resolution of approval for the use of troops, rather than trying to impose its unformed will by inaction.

2. Authority of a "Core Group." Congress as a deliberative body ought not to delegate its ultimate authority to any committee. But the core group envisioned in the Byrd-Nunn version of this proposal would not have ultimate authority. In sending this group to consult with the administration about national security, Congress would be recognizing that modern conditions sometimes require a degree of secrecy and speed that a bicameral body of 535 members cannot produce. But it would retain the ultimate authority to sanction the use of military force in extended operations, and it ought to agree to impose upon itself the discipline of expedited procedures in order to give its decision, pro or con, in a timely fashion.

3. Voluntary Information Sharing. It would certainly be preferable if presidents would share the war powers with Congress voluntarily. But we cannot rely on voluntary cooperation. As Madison wrote in *The Federalist,* number 51, "If men were angels, no government would be necessary." If presidents could be trusted to consider all sides of the issue before committing troops to battle, safeguards would not be necessary.

4. The Framers' Intent. The framers could not have foreseen the effect that permanent armies would have on the president's powers as commander in chief. If they had, they would have insisted on other safeguards against monarchical war powers. Now that such armies have come into being, we must make the adjustments ourselves.

5. *Divided Control.* The framers' insistence that the president share the war powers with Congress did not stem from a belief that members of Congress would be wiser than presidents or their advisers. Nor does the modern case for meaningful consultation depend on a belief that members of Congress are wiser than presidents or cabinet members. Senator Claiborne Pell, chair of the Senate Foreign Relations Committee, may or may not be smarter or more experienced than Secretary of State James Baker; Representative Les Aspin, chair of the House Armed Services Committee, may or may not be better informed about military preparedness than Secretary of Defense Dick Cheney. The essential difference is that the senators and representatives serve in Congress at the pleasure of their constituents, and in leadership positions in Congress at the pleasure of their colleagues, not the president.

The importance of this point was underscored when Secretary of State George Shultz revealed that he had considered resigning from President Reagan's cabinet when his opposition to the Iran-contra scheme was ignored or overridden. He decided not to resign, so that he could continue to work on other issues.

The political calculation for a member of Congress would be different. He or she would have to think how a given action would appear to the public and to other politicians if it ever saw the light of day, and how his colleagues and constituents would view it. His ultimate political loyalties would lie elsewhere; his instinct for political survival would weigh the factors differently.

The framers' intent was that the war powers should not be invoked unless they survived scrutiny in a given case from several distinct angles of vision. Thus, they insisted the "dog of war" should not be unleashed without the concurrence of both branches.

Arguments Against This Proposal

1. Judging the Resolution. The WPR has predictably failed, and it ought to be repealed, not amended. It seeks to encode a relationship which the Constitution wisely leaves to the interaction of political forces.

In giving Congress control over the creation and provisioning of armed forces, they guaranteed that the people's representatives could not be left out of any serious military encounter. Presidents who neglect to inform Congress of their plans eventually suffer from a lack of popular support, which quickly translates into effective political opposition. But the same framers gave the president control over the use of armed force, because they understood that Congress, a body of 535 divergent people, could not act with the requisite vigor and dispatch.

We have admittedly suffered from presidential abuse of war powers, but we have also suffered from congressional attempts to micro-manage foreign policy. The separation and balancing of powers does not guarantee sound policy. But it does enable each branch to promote its point of view and defend its assigned turf.

2. Authority of a "Core Group." Who speaks for Congress? By this proposal, a group of leaders are expected to do so. But such a procedure violates the spirit of the Constitution. These people will be asked to act like executives, sharing secrets they cannot divulge and joining in decisions without fully consulting their colleagues. Then, whereas they might otherwise have criticized the administration's course of action from outside, either they will be coopted, or they will divide the counsels of government.

3. Voluntary Information Sharing. Presidents cannot be forced to share their war powers. Most presidents want to consult broadly before taking military action, and they will take good counsel wherever they find it. But if they are convinced that certain individuals who occupy leadership positions in Congress are fools or untrustworthy, they will find a way around them. If a president finds such persons in the "core group," those consultations will be pro forma, and real consultations will take place elsewhere. If he is forced to choose members of Congress to serve on the NSC, and he feels he must act in ways that would be opposed by these people, he will find other ways to get his work done, as Roosevelt did when he was confronted in 1939 by members of Congress who opposed his determination that we must prepare for war.

4. The Framers' Intent. We should always be wary of reforms based on the argument that the framers were naive. The framers had lived through a harrowing war for independence, and they had three dangerous foes in Britain, Spain and France, not to mention the warriors of native American tribes. Nor were they opposed in principle to a standing army in all circumstances.[19]

Even though we now have permanent military forces, Congress can exert pressure on the administration by setting conditions on their use. Presidents have not acted on personal whim. Most applications of armed force have been consistent with our treaty obligations.

5. Divided Control. It is beside the point to compare the wisdom of public officials. The Constitution makes the president commander in chief because one person can act with the requisite vigor and speed better than 535 people. Napoleon once said that he would rather have one bad general than two good ones in charge of his troops. We must be careful not to divide the councils that direct our armed forces.

You Decide

☐ Is it constitutional and wise to force the president to share his war powers? Do modern conditions—intercontinental missiles, nuclear weapons, instant telecommunications—make it impractical for the president to share these powers with Congress?

☐ Can members of Congress be trusted with national security secrets?

REQUIRING A BALANCED BUDGET

The Existing Situation

The Constitution provides that no money may be spent by the federal government except in consequence of an appropriation enacted into law. To generate income, Congress has power to lay and collect taxes and to borrow money on the credit of the United States. The Constitution also requires that "a regular statement and account of the receipts and expenditures of all public money shall be published from time to time." But there is no requirement in the Constitution that Congress limit expenditures to the amount of revenues generated in any given year.

The Basic Proposal

RESOLVED: That the Constitution should be amended to require that Congress enact an annual budget in which revenues and expenditures are balanced, unless three-fifths of Congress votes in favor of a motion to enact an unbalanced budget for a given year.

Discussion

The budget is currently so far out of balance that most people, even those who favor a balanced budget amendment, believe that we would need to phase in a constitutional commitment to a balanced budget over a period of years.

Some people have suggested that we could move toward a balanced budget by giving the president the item veto, that is, power to strike particular items from an appropriations act without vetoing the whole measure. This power might perhaps be given without a constitutional amendment, if Congress and the president were able to enact a procedure into law.

Nearly everyone agrees that a loophole is necessary to enable the government in time of war or national emergency to meet extraordinary expenses. But the loophole provision can be varied (raising or lowering the necessary majority)) to make it easier or more difficult to suspend the requirement that the budget be balanced.

Relevant Facts

☐ Over the course of the twentieth century, budget surpluses and deficits have varied enormously. The last time there was a series of budget surpluses was during the 1920s, when we were paying off the debt for World War I. During the 1930s, expenditures on programs to counteract the Great Depression sometimes drove deficits to totals that were higher than the federal government's receipts for the year. Again during World War II (1941–1945), expenditures were more than twice as high as revenues, adding enormously to the national debt. Then, during the Truman and Eisenhower administrations, there was a slight surplus; in fact, from the end of World War II until the Vietnam War (excluding 1959), annual federal budgets were nearly in balance every year.

Since the close of the Vietnam War, deficits exceeded 3 percent of the gross national product in 1976 and in each year between 1982 and 1987. The effect of these deficits has been to push the national debt to unprecedented heights. In 1981, the accumulated national debt stood at just under $1 trillion. By 1989, it had more than doubled, to a total of $2.8 trillion.

The level of national debt is important because we must use current revenues to pay interest on it. Thus, if we buy something today without raising revenues to pay for it, we must borrow money, and then we (or our children) must pay interest on the money we have borrowed until we retire the debt. Interest is an inescapable cost; it cannot normally be deferred.

Assuming interest rates of 10 percent, a national debt of $3 trillion consumes $300 billion in revenues annually.

☐ James Buchanan, who won the Nobel Prize for economic science in 1986, argues that the willingness to incur debt is a relatively recent phenomenon. Until the 1930s, he contends, Americans believed that it was immoral for the government, or anyone else, to spend more money than it had or could raise in a given year. Along came John Maynard Keynes, the British economic theorist, who held that the insistence on balancing national budgets every year was wooden-headed, that deficits had a stimulating effect and could be useful to lift an economy out of recession. Keynes added that surpluses were sometimes useful, too, to restrain an economy that was running toward inflation. Buchanan argues that modern democracies delightedly accepted Keynes's call for stimulation by deficit spending, but were politically incapable of enacting surpluses when they were needed or of balancing budgets over the long haul, as Keynes's theory required. Buchanan concludes that, since Keynesian thinking has undermined the moral principle that guided economic policy-making until the 1930s, we must now build that discipline into the Constitution itself.[20]

☐ Other economists disagree with Buchanan. Robert Eisner, who has served as president of the American Economic Association, calls attention to proportions: deficits as a percentage of gross national product. By that standard, he argues, recent deficits are not so bad. Further, he argues that we must distinguish different kinds of expenditures and recognize that investments in productive assets will help us to expand our revenue base in future years, whereas cuts may diminish our capacity to raise revenues in the future.[21]

☐ Some people (such as Dick Thornburgh, formerly governor of Pennsylvania, now attorney general in the Bush administration) argue that we should produce separate budgets for capital investments. That way, the government would have a more accurate picture of the impact of governmental revenues and expenditures on the national economy in a given year. If we did that, argues Thornburgh, it would make more sense to require that the rest of the budget (including interest payments) be balanced.

☐ As of 1987, 32 state legislatures had adopted resolutions calling upon Congress to call a federal convention for the purpose of proposing an amendment requiring a balanced federal budget. Article V of the Constitution directs that Congress must call such a convention whenever three-quarters of the states (that is, 34) so resolve. Questions have been raised about the legal standing of some of these resolutions, but the existence of so many of them has brought pressure on Congress to meet the demand for a balanced budget.

☐ In 1986, Congress enacted a plan for cutting the annual federal deficit to zero over a five-year period. Named for its sponsors (Senators Phil Gramm [Republican, Texas], Warren Rudman [Republican, New Hampshire] and Fritz Hollings [Democrat, South Carolina]), the law set a series of ceilings on the annual deficit which descended to zero over a five-year period. If the budget passed by Congress failed to meet the statutory ceiling for a given year, the law empowered the controller general to impose cuts on expenditures across the board (with exemptions for certain programs such as social security, medicaid, veterans benefits, and food stamps).

In 1986, the Supreme Court, in *Bowsher vs. Synar* (106 S. Ct. 3181), ruled that the enforcement mechanism of Gramm-Rudman-Hollings was unconstitutional, because it gave executive power to an official who was independent of presidential control and answerable primarily to Congress. Since that decision, the Gramm-Rudman-Hollings ceilings have had moral authority only, and Congress has not been able to meet them.

☐ Public opinion surveys on this question have been volatile. In 1982, political lines seemed to be drawn fairly clearly between a president anxious to cut spending and Congress protecting domestic social programs. In that atmosphere, 74 percent favored a balanced budget amendment to the Constitution, 17 percent were opposed, and 9 percent had no opinion. By 1987, the president had submitted a series of unbalanced budgets himself, and we had prospered for several years despite the deficits. That year, 53 percent were favorable to the amendment, 23 percent opposed, and 24 percent had no opinion.[22]

☐ Twice in recent years, a balanced budget amendment has moved toward enactment in Congress. In 1982, the Senate passed a version, but it died in the House. In 1986, the Senate killed a proposed amendment by a single vote. The final tally was 66-34, one vote short of the necessary two-thirds majority. It was opposed by 24 Democratic senators and ten Republicans.

Arguments in Favor of This Proposal

1. Incurring Debts. It is immoral to run up debts that our children must pay. We should live within our means. Apparently we lack the moral fibre to do it voluntarily, so the Constitution should require it of us, just as most state constitutions do.

2. Raising Revenues. In balancing budgets, there is no need to confine our efforts to the expenditure side. If Congress and the president were required to achieve a balanced budget, the logic of the situation would force them to work out a strategy that combined cuts in spending with increased revenues.

3. Maintaining Fiscal Discipline. Whether or not our political system is working well, and whether or not we can ever agree to change it, we need to stop piling up deficits. Experience in recent years proves that the only way we can do that is to mandate it in the Constitution.

4. An Economic Theory in the Constitution. Balancing budgets is not an economic theory; it is plain common sense. The people of this land know that we have been living beyond our means, and they believe that we should stop it. Besides, the amendment would not be a straitjacket; it would contain a loophole for emergencies. What we must stop is the tendency to overspend in normal times, and there is no good economic reason not just to prohibit it.

Arguments Against This Proposal

1. Incurring Debts. Debts run up during the 1980s may well have been excessive, but the household analogy can help us to understand that debt by itself is not necessarily bad. Even in households, we incur debt in order to afford things we need but cannot pay for all at once. We acquire homes with mortgage loans. So long as we have a good income, we can sustain the payments on these loans. We need to be careful not to take on more indebtedness than we can service, but it is foolish to insist that all debt is bad.

2. Raising Revenues. The principal trouble with most efforts to require a balanced budget is that they impose their disciplines only on the expenditure side. That was the way Gramm-Rudman-Hollings worked: If the budget was not balanced, cut expenditures. But a budget consists of expenditures and revenues. And as David Stockman, President Reagan's chief adviser on the federal budget, insisted in his memoir, the only way we are ever going to balance the federal budget is to raise taxes.[23]

3. Maintaining Fiscal Discipline. The real question is: How are we going to restore fiscal discipline? We lack fiscal responsibility because the branches of the government are controlled by opposing parties. Rather than working together to develop a responsible budget, they indulge in political posturing. As Lloyd Cutler has pointed out, we have not had large deficits since World War II when the same party has controlled both branches of the government.

4. An Economic Theory in the Constitution. A constitutional mandate for a balanced budget would be an economic straitjacket. It would enshrine an economic theory in the Constitution. Economists disagree about the need for balanced budgets in different circumstances. We must work out these matters in the give and take of the political process, just as we have for two hundred years.

You Decide

☐ Does our political process lead us to behave in a way that is fiscally unsound?

☐ Would a balanced budget amendment be too inflexible? Would it tend to put undue pressure on the expenditure side of the budgetary equation?

9
What We Do When Government Fails

DISSOLVING THE GOVERNMENT AND HOLDING SPECIAL ELECTIONS

The Existing Situation

The Constitution establishes fixed terms of office for members of the House of Representatives (two years), for senators (six years), and for the president and vice-president (four years). It provides that members of the House and Senate may be expelled from office only by the concurrence of two-thirds of the members of their chamber. (In 1797, a senator from Tennessee, William Blount, was expelled for his involvement in a scheme to transfer control of Spanish Florida and Louisiana to Great Britain.) As for the president, he is secure in office for his full four-year term unless he is impeached (by majority vote of the House) and convicted (by two-thirds vote in the Senate) of "treason, bribery, or other high crimes and misdemeanors." If impeached and convicted, he is removed from office. Only one president, Andrew Johnson in 1868, has been impeached; the Senate voted 35-19 for conviction, one vote short of the two-thirds majority necessary to remove Johnson from office.

In the only other case of a president facing possible impeachment, President Nixon resigned from office in August, 1974, before the House could vote on impeachment articles prepared by its Committee on the Judiciary.

The Basic Proposal

RESOLVED: That we need a mechanism by which the people, in special elections, can pass judgment on a stalemated or disabled government, either by confirming incumbents in office or electing replacements.

Discussion

To introduce a power of dissolution into our political system, it would be necessary to amend the Constitution. The simplest way to do it would be to provide that the president, by proclamation, could call for national elections at any time during his term of office; so could Congress, by concurrent resolution (requiring a majority vote in both houses, but not the president's signature). If such a proclamation or resolution were issued, elections would follow within sixty days; at stake in the elections would be the presidency and vice-presidency, all seats in the House, and one of the two senatorial seats from each state. Winning candidates would begin full terms within fourteen days after the election.

Possible Variations

☐ An amendment to provide a power of dissolution could be shaped in various ways. In choosing between these alternatives, we would have to adjust the balances very carefully.

We might, for example, want to temper the president's power to threaten Congress with dissolution. If so, instead of a simple procla-mation by the president, we could require that the president gain the concurrence of a certain proportion of the Congress (say, a majority of either house, or one-third of both chambers) before issuing the proclamation.

Or, if we wanted to avoid giving too much power to a hostile partisan majority in Congress, we might provide that a call for new elections would require majorities in both houses, as well as the president's signature, or two-thirds majorities in both houses to override a presidential veto.

Another option would be to make it easier to call for elections. If so, perhaps a majority in just one house could do so.[1]

☐ Similarly, we could adjust the length of the period between the official call for the election and the balloting. Under present practices, it takes many months for parties to choose their candidates and conduct their campaigns. If our amendment required that the elections be held within a short time (six or eight weeks) of the formal decision to proceed with them, it would force parties to compress their nominating processes. That might be a desireable change in and of itself. But we ought not to be unrealistic. We would need to think carefully about the repercussions, if our amendment seemed likely to force an alteration in current campaign practices.

☐ We might want language in the amendment to specify the circumstances that would justify a decision to take the government to the nation. For example, we might require that the proclamation or resolution assert a lack of confidence in the other branch, or a finding that the branches were stalemated on an issue of fundamental importance. Or we might prefer to omit any statement of the circumstances that compelled new elections and rely instead on the procedures to prevent abuses.

☐ Whose seats should be at stake in the event of special elections?

Some have held that the power of dissolution should be given to the president alone. By this reasoning, presidents would be unlikely to abuse the power by calling unnecessary or fruitless elections. If a president called an election in which the result was the reelection of the incumbents, he would pay for his miscalculation by having to face an emboldened opposition.

Others contend that what we really need is to broaden the power of Congress to remove presidents who abuse their powers or lose the capacity to govern. We might do this by broadening the power of impeachment, allowing Congress to vacate the presidency on a finding that the country had lost confidence in his leadership. This would permit the timely termination of a totally failed or discredited presidency. (If the people did not agree with the congressional judgment, it might reelect the incumbent. The fear of such an outcome would presumably temper the temptation in Congress to play political games.)

The proposal outlined above rejects these alternatives. It rests on the view that dissolution ought not to be seen constitutionally as punishment, but rather as recognition that the government is bogged down and needs renewal, for whatever reason.

☐ In the event of a special election, ought the newly elected officials to serve new, full terms, or should they simply complete the balance of the terms for which they were originally elected? To avoid overly frequent elections and to give the new government a chance to prove itself, we opt here for new full terms.

☐ Should there be a time limit on calling special elections? Should we require that they cannot be called during the first, or last, year of a president's term, or should we set a specific "window" within which Congress might consider a resolution for special national elections?

As a practical matter, the likelihood of invoking dissolution and calling special elections would be low during the honeymoon at the beginning of a presidential term (unless the outcome of the election cast doubt on the president's legitimacy, in which case a new election might not be a bad idea), and also as the term neared completion. Furthermore, setting a specific window might invite speculation where none was justified.

Relevant Facts

☐ We normally associate dissolution with parliamentary systems. In Great Britain, for example, there is no written constitution, but the laws provide that elections must be held within five years after the seating of a new parliament. In Canada and France, there must be parliamentary elections within five years; in West Germany, within four years. In parliamentary countries, whenever the legal time limit is reached, or it is no longer possible for a cabinet to gain support from existing members of parliament, whichever comes first, government is dissolved and the nation proceeds to new elections.

To see how this system of dissolution works, take Britain, the "mother of parliaments," as an example. As prime minister, Margaret Thatcher may ask Queen Elizabeth to dissolve parliament and call elections whenever she (Mrs. Thatcher) chooses. If her party has a comfortable majority in Parliament and things go well, she is likely to wait for a politically favorable opportunity toward the end of the five-year cycle. If her majority is shaky, or if the opposition is off-balance, she may dissolve Parliament and call elections sooner than that. If serious political trouble were to develop, she might be forced to concede that she could no longer govern, in which case she would submit her resignation to the monarch. At that point, the monarch, acting on the advice of leading politicians, would decide whether a different prime minister could create a stable and effective government from the existing members of Parliament. If not, she would call new parliamentary elections.

Italy is an example of a parliamentary system in which the prime minister has often been forced to concede (to the president, otherwise a largely ceremonial official in Italy) that he is no longer able to govern. That is because Italy has a multi-party system, with no single dominant party. Prime ministers must form coalitions when they put together their cabinets. But coalitions are unstable. Partners try to exact a price for their support; finally the prime minister is no longer able to satisfy everyone in his cabinet and his government "falls." But the president, realizing that new elections are likely to produce a similar parliamentary line-up, waits to see if a new coalition forms. Only as a last resort (or if the legal time limit is at hand) will he call new elections. Thus, between the end of World War II and 1987, Italy had forty-five "governments" (that is, forty-five separate cabinets that assumed responsibility for obtaining support in parliament for the policies of the government), but only ten national parliamentary elections.[2]

☐ Many people throughout American history (mostly academics and journalists, not many politicians) have proposed that the United States adopt some form of the parliamentary system. Perhaps the fullest expression of the idea came in a book by William MacDonald, *A New Constitution for America* (B. W. Huebsch, 1921). MacDonald's model would have reduced the presidency to a ceremonial office, save for the responsibility of selecting a "premier" from Congress, who would head a cabinet consisting of other members of Congress and would resign whenever his cabinet lost the confidence of both houses. Woodrow Wilson, as a young political scientist, wrote several critiques of the American constitutional system in which his preference for Britain's parliamentary system is clear. More recently, Professor Charles Hardin (in *Presidential Power and Accountability: Toward a New Constitution* [University of Chicago Press, 1974]), C. Douglas Dillon (in his commencement address at Tufts University in 1982) and J. William Fulbright (in *The Price of Empire* [Pantheon, 1989]) have indicated interest in the parliamentary model as a source of ideas that might help to relieve American problems.[3]

☐ Why did the framers establish fixed terms? Judging from *The Federalist,* the principal reason was to insulate officials from popular passions. In number 63, Madison argues that the six-year term of senators is needed to enable them to resist the "temporary errors and delusions" of the people; in number 71, Hamilton argues that a four-year term will insure "the personal firmness of the executive magistrate." Both Madison and Hamilton affirm that the will of the people ought ultimately to prevail in "republican" governments, but both insist that it is sometimes necessary for elected officials to withstand a "sudden breeze of passion" blowing through the body politic. Fixed terms of sufficient duration fortify them.

Arguments in Favor of This Proposal

1. Insulated Presidency. The framers, in their anxiety to protect the president from political reprisal and to seal off the administration from the corrupting influence of Congress, created a potential monster. The United States is the only constitutional democracy in the world that has no means—short of convicting the president himself of "treason, bribery, or other high crimes and misdemeanors"—of removing an administration that is corrupt or has shown itself incompetent and inadequate to the challenges facing the nation. As James Sundquist has written, "With the democratization of the presidential selection process and the growth of executive power, the fixity of a president in office for four full years, no matter how incompetent he may prove to be, is a weakness in the American system that can, in a time of grave emergency, be perilous. For a president to be merely nontreasonous and noncriminal is no longer enough, if it ever was."[4]

2. Impeachment as a Remedy. Impeachment is a totally inadequate remedy for most of the ills that befall our government.[5] It is, in the first place, a judicial process, unsuited to a test of political principles and an assessment of performance in office. It is too slow, and it directs attention to fine points in the law, rather than to a broad consideration of principles and fitness for office.

Furthermore, its outcome is inappropriate for cases in which the president has been accused of maladministration. If convicted by the Senate, a president is succeeded by his hand-picked vice-president, and there need not be any other changes in the administration.

Note also that impeachment does not reach the case where the deadlock, the conflict between the branches, is Congress's fault. We cannot rejuvenate Congress by impeachment. Where the branches are locked in conflict over fundamental issues, the people ought to judge.

3. Influence on Parties. It is true that American political parties, in their present form, would not be able to make nominations and conduct their campaigns within the time limits set by the proposal, but parties take their form from the constitutional system in which they find themselves. If the system held the possibility of elections on short notice, parties would adjust. They might want to have their nominees ready on a standing basis. Such a "loyal opposition" might conduct a running critique of the government and stand before the public as a definite alternative to the existing regime.

4. Independence of Congress. Providing for dissolution and special elections would not, as might be imagined, give us a parliamentary system. The key to a parliamentary system is the fusion of executive and legislative powers, and the dominant party or coalition in parliament chooses the prime minister. In our system, Congress and the president would continue to be chosen separately. Congress, separately elected, would continue to be independent, each member answering to a local constituency.

5. Breaking Deadlocks. Our system promotes government by finger-pointing. Take the deficit, for example. Everyone deplores it, but no one accepts responsibility. The president blames Congress; Congress blames the administration. Both claim to represent the people's wishes, but the voters are not able to render a clear verdict.

If there were a provision for dissolution and new elections, the president could present to Congress a plan for reducing the deficit. If Congress blocked it, he could dissolve the government and take the issue to the nation. Then we would find out whether the voters sided with the president and his plan or with Congress and its resistance. If the electoral verdict were unclear, we would know that the public had not made up its mind.

6. *Stability.* The virtue of "stability" in our present arrangements must be balanced against their rigidity in the face of crisis. We do not want a hair-trigger on the device that keeps our government accountable and responsive. But neither can we afford a government that is impervious to deadlock or disaster.

7. *Influence on Incumbency.* It is true that elections following a dissolution may not resolve the crisis. The voters may return the same politicians to office and let the deadlock continue. But if they did, it would weaken the claim that the president represented the people's desire for a decisive departure.

Also, a mechanism of this kind, tying elections to political crises, might weaken the tendency to re-elect incumbents. One reason that incumbents tend to win reelection so often is that campaigns often occur in relatively tranquil times. Dissolution signals a crisis. It would not happen unless someone thought the people were ready for a change.

8. *Effects on Campaigning.* The only way to shorten campaigns and reduce their cost, so long as the First Amendment protects free speech and unlimited expenditures for political campaigns, is to make it uncertain when elections will be held. Politicians now aim at a particular campaign months or even years in advance. If no one knew the date of the next election, parties would have to be ready for a campaign at any time, but they could not sustain a campaign perpetually.

Arguments Against This Proposal

1. *Insulated Presidency.* The framers' decision to fix the president's term and insulate his tenure in office from political reprisal was the shrewdest, most farseeing thing they did in 1787. It gave the government a stable administration and provided strength at the center of executive power, something other constitutional democracies have sometimes coveted. France, for example, has finally abandoned a purely parliamentary system, instituting in 1958 a presidency insulated, like ours,

from parliamentary maneuvers. The need for strength and stability, particularly in foreign relations and in command of military forces, led the modern French framers to adopt features quite similar to our own separation of powers.

But the American executive power is not just stable and strong. It is also constrained in many ways: by legislation and by congressional control over the purse strings, by independent courts, by the hectoring of a free press. What we have is a system of coequal branches, separated and exquisitely balanced, and it has served us well, adapting with remarkable sensitivity to the changes wrought by the years.

2. *Impeachment as a Remedy.* The impeachment process is not a "rusty musket in the closet," as the late Edward S. Corwin used to say. It helped to bring President Nixon down, less than two years after one of the great landslide victories in American history. If we had rushed to judgment in that case, we might never have known the full extent of that administration's crimes. No merely political process could have done so thorough and unanswerable a job; no one could have pronounced, as definitively as President Ford did in his inaugural address, "Our long national nightmare is over." The process is indeed slow, but it is also satisfying in a way that no merely political conflict can be.

As for resolving deadlocks between the branches: When the people truly want action, the politicians in the two branches will feel the pressure and move to compromise on the issues that have produced the impasse. An appeal to the people, through elections in which incumbents faced off against challengers, would probably return many of the same people to office, and soon they too would fall into a similar pattern of opposition.

3. *Influence on Parties.* We ought not to try to force American political parties into this procrustean bed. What's wrong with a system where everyone knows the rules and timetable in advance? We have finally developed a system that allows voters to participate in the nominating process through primary elections. It takes time, but it is a truly democratic exercise. We should steer clear of any "reforms" that threaten to undo the democratization of the electoral process.

4. *Independence of Congress.* Americans do not want a parliamentary system—not all of it, and not any significant part of it. The American Congress is the envy of every legislative body in the world. Its independence and strength are precious assets. The effect of dissolution would be to make congressional elections subservient to presidential elections. (The converse situation would be no better. We do not want

a president who is the plaything of the barons on Capitol Hill.) Let us not tinker with the balances we have: they work well.

5. *Breaking Deadlocks.* Elections in a republic are not referenda. When we vote for presidents or members of Congress, we are not determining the details of public policy. At most, we are indicating broad directions, to the extent that they are embodied in a particular candidate. But the basic decision is about the character of the candidates. When we tie elections too closely to particular issues (as would tend to be the case if dissolution were introduced into our system), we ask the electorate to make decisions for which it is ill-equipped.

6. *Stability.* A dissolution mechanism would be destabilizing. The president would be afraid to make bold and unpopular decisions. (Imagine President Truman in 1947, confronted by a Republican majority in Congress. Would he not have had to proceed far more cautiously?) The congressional leadership, for its part, would likewise hesitate to resist a popular president. (What would have happened if President Nixon had aborted the Watergate inquiry by dissolving the government and taking his case to the nation before Congress had been able to prepare the evidence against him?)

7. *Influence on Incumbency.* It is most likely, given recent rates of reelection for congressional incumbents, that a special election would return the same crew to Washington and renew the same old quarrels. If the nation has really made up its mind about an issue, we do not need an election to establish that fact. It would be communicated to politicians, who are nothing if not sensitive to shifts in the wind.

8. *Effects on Campaigning.* We should not try to escape from the First Amendment protections for the length and cost of campaigns. They are an instrinsic part of American democracy. We grouse about the length of campaigns, but we reward politicians who start early and stay the course. That is because we know that voters need time to examine the candidates and study the issues. As for the cost, there are more direct, less destructive ways to deal with that problem.

You Decide

☐ Is the impeachment process an adequate mechanism for dealing with the kinds of abuses of presidential power that we may have to face in the years ahead?

☐ Would it be possible to devise a provision for special elections that would maintain (or restore) the proper balance between presidential and congressional power?

☐ Could our parties adjust to a system that allowed for elections outside the regular two- and four-year cycle?

PROVIDING A NATIONAL REFERENDUM

The Existing Situation

There is no provision in the Constitution for "direct legislation"— that is, for the enactment of laws directly by the electorate. Many states, particularly those west of the Mississippi, conduct referendums; California has made extensive use of the device. But the United States is "one of the very few democratic countries that has never had a referendum at the national level."[6]

The Basic Proposal

RESOLVED: That the Constitution should be amended to provide for the enactment of federal laws by referendum.

Discussion

A *referendum* is an arrangement whereby a piece of legislation, having been passed or proposed by a legislature, does not go into force until it has been approved directly by the people (in some specified proportion) in a general election. An *initiative* is a procedure enabling a specified number of voters by petition to propose a law or constitutional amendment and secure its submission to the electorate for approval. It too becomes law when affirmed by a majority (or special majority) of voters in a general election. The proposal under debate here calls for a national referendum.

Possible Variations

☐ An amendment to provide for a national referendum would need to stipulate the majority that would be required to enact any bill submitted to the national electorate. It might be a simple majority of those voting on the proposal (as in California), or it might (as in Switzerland and Australia) be a majority of the total electorate. Under the Weimar Republic in Germany (in the 1920s), two referendums supported by over 90 percent of the voters failed to be adopted because the turnout was so low that the aye votes did not amount to a majority of the electorate.[7]

☐ It is possible to restrict referendums to certain categories of legislation and to prohibit any referendum on certain subjects, such as a declaration of war or matters relating to the Bill of Rights.

☐ Sometimes referendums are only advisory. They seek an authoritative statement of public opinion on a question, but do not enact anything. For example, in Great Britain in 1975, there was a referendum on the question of whether Britain should stay in the European Economic Community. It was the only referendum the British have ever conducted. Though not a piece of legislation, it produced a decisive affirmative vote (67.2 percent voted yes, on a turnout of 64.5 percent) and helped to resolve a muddle in British politics.[8]

Relevant Facts

☐ The first referendum in modern history was the one by which the people of Massachusetts ratified their new constitution in 1778. As of 1978, forty-nine states (all except Delaware) required that constitutional amendments be approved by referendum. Thirty-nine states provided for the approval of statutes by referendum, and twenty-two provided for statutes by initiative. In addition, many localities have procedures for legislation by referendum and initiative. A study in 1970 estimated that there were as many as ten to fifteen thousand referendums annually in America, most of them at the local level.[9]

During this century, referendums and initiatives have been used to secure women's suffrage, to levy and to cap taxes, to enact right-to-work laws, to impose the death penalty, to prohibit busing to achieve racial balance in public schools, to regulate nuclear power, and, in 1972, "to prohibit the State [of Colorado] from levying taxes and appropriating or loaning funds for the purpose of aiding or furthering the 1976 Winter Olympic Games." The latter, an initiative, attracted an affirmative vote of 59 percent, and the Games had to be moved to Innsbruck, Austria.[10]

☐ The record is unclear as to whether direct legislation tends to favor liberal or conservative political causes. Progressives in the early twentieth century pushed for the device, but in recent years, conservatives, believing that most ordinary Americans are basically conservative, have often used referendums as a way of bypassing a political process dominated, as they see it, by the liberal media.

Attempting an objective assessment, political scientist Austin Ranney studied all state referendums between 1945 and 1976 that involved clear liberal-conservative choices. Adding together "apples and oranges," he found a score of 24 victories for conservatives and 19 for liberals.

Further analysis showed that on economic questions, liberals generally won; on social issues, conservatives; and on nuclear power issues, environmentalists broke about even with advocates of economic growth. He concluded that "the referendum is neither an unfailing friend nor an implacable enemy of either left or right."[11]

☐ In 1977, Senator James Abourezk (Democrat, South Dakota) proposed to amend the Constitution by providing a method for setting legislation before the voters by popular petition. The petition would have to be signed by voters equal in number to 3 percent of the ballots in the previous presidential election (in 1978, the number would have been 2,446,677), and by at least 3 percent of the voters in ten different states. It would have exempted from enactment by initiative constitutional amendments, declarations of war, and calling up the militia. Proposals would be put on the ballot at the next congressional election after qualifying. If favored by a majority of voters in that election, a bill would become law in thirty days. For two years thereafter, it could be repealed only by two-thirds of both houses of Congress; after that, it would be subject to ordinary congressional majorities. Abourezk's proposal found two influential sponsors in the House (Guy Vander Jagt, Republican, Michigan, and James Jones, Democrat, Oklahoma), and it was favored by 57 percent in a Gallup poll (21 percent were opposed). But it never made much headway in Congress.[12]

Arguments in Favor of This Proposal

1. Direct Versus Representative Democracy. America's deepest commitment is to self-government, "government of the people, by the people, for the people." What process can realize this ideal more purely, more completely, than direct legislation? Because of the size of the country, we have resorted to representative democracy for most purposes. On great occasions, however, we ought to be able to use a process that lets the people decide the fundamental issues. That is the American tradition: town-meeting democracy, face-to-face in the assembly room. Direct legislation is the closest modern equivalent.

2. Overcoming Voter Apathy. We worry about a low turnout on election day. People are not voting because they see little or no connection between their vote and what happens afterwards. If they had a chance to vote directly on legislation, there would be no intermediary steps. Votes would have immediate consequences.

3. Curing the Ills of Democracy. Usually the government in this country works pretty well, but sometimes the legislative mills get clogged and pressure groups monopolize the attention of elected officials. When this happens, grass roots citizens need to bypass the system in order to accomplish their purposes. As the Progressive slogan put it, "The only cure for the ills of democracy is more democracy."

4. The Legislative Process. Nobody thinks that ordinary citizens, by direct legislation, can frame a complicated tax code, or reform the agricultural price-support system, or work out the details of a revenue-sharing scheme. What they can do is set limits and force action, in accordance with their deepest values and beliefs.

5. Elections Versus Polls. Public opinion polls are no substitute for elections. The answer one gives to an interviewer who unexpectedly poses a question is not the same as the vote one casts after a long campaign on an issue. Polls in Britain that attempted to measure public sentiment toward the Common Market fluctuated wildly in the years before the 1975 referendum, all the way from a 44 point plurality for entry (1966) to a 42 point plurality against (1970).[13] If we really care what the people think about an issue, we should put it straight to them on election day.

Arguments Against This Proposal

1. Direct Versus Representative Democracy. The United States is a republic, not a direct democracy. Lincoln's great formula characterized the American government under the Constitution. We do not "resort" to representation; we regard it as a positive virtue of our system of government. Ours is a government by consent of the governed. The people's will is indeed sovereign, but we are not simple-minded in the way we go about ascertaining what it is.

2. Overcoming Voter Apathy. We will not overcome voter apathy by pretending that voters can govern the country by direct legislation. Other countries that have high turnout rates use direct legislation only rarely, if ever (Britain, for example, only once, and that on an advisory vote). It is not referendums that draw people to the polls in the other democracies. It is the prospect of passing judgment on the performance of the government, of deciding whether to continue with the existing government or turn the reins over to the opposition. That is a judgment the people can make, and it firmly guides the course of government, far more so than a sporadic piece of direct legislation.

3. Curing the Ills of Democracy. Referendums are not a means to overcome the influence of pressure groups. In California, for example, well-heeled interest groups wage fierce campaigns in the media and use every trick in the book to influence the outcome. The common citizen has no chance to be heard in this maelstrom and little hope of mastering the many issues that appear on the ballot.

4. The Legislative Process. The legislative process is extremely sensitive to popular opinion. In addition, it respects the intensity of people's feelings on an issue—something that a straight yes-or-no vote cannot do. And it respects the rights of minorities, far better than referendums do. The English philosopher, Ernest Barker, put it well:

> Discussion is not only like war; it is also like love. It is not only a battle of ideas; it is also a marriage of minds. If a majority engages in discussion with a minority, and if that discussion is conducted in a spirit of giving and taking, the result will be that the ideas of the majority are widened to include some of the ideas of the minority which have established their truth in the give and take of debate. When this happens, the will of the majority will not be the abstract or isolated will of a mere majority. . . . Some fusion will have taken place; some accommodation will have been attained.[14]

Referendums not only short-circuit the legislative process; they also undermine it. The prospect of direct legislation makes legislators wary. Why wrestle with tough issues when you can pass the buck to the electorate? Why make hard choices when someone who disagrees with the outcome in Congress can take the issue to a referendum?

5. Elections Versus Polls. There are other means of taking the pulse of public opinion. There are public opinion polls, and legislators have their own means of gathering the people's views.

You Decide

☐ Do we need a more direct way for citizens to express their will?

☐ If we allow it at all, should the opportunity for direct legislation be confined to certain issues? What kind of majority should be required?

☐ Would the opportunity for direct legislation undermine representative government? Would we be tempted to resort to it too often?

10
How Reforms Interact

The American political system is an organism whose many parts interact in intricate ways. That is one of the reasons that reforms of the system often have unintended consequences.

The fact that reforms are difficult to control is no reason to flinch from facing our problems and taking steps to correct them. Those who offer such counsel are telling us to sit quietly and wait for the end. Americans will not do that. Ours is an active tradition. We have made mistakes, from the founding generation to our own, and we will make more, but we will not give up the quest for a "more perfect union."

At the same time, it behooves us to think as carefully as we can about the changes we propose to make. We need to be "wise as serpents, and harmless as doves." We should study carefully whether reforms are needed and, if so, how radical they need to be. (We ought not to assume that minor changes—tinkering—is preferable to basic reforms because it is less harmful. If our problems are serious, we may need major reforms. If not, we probably ought not to tinker.) We should think carefully about where reforms are likely to take us, and whether we ought to consider certain steps in combination in order to preserve the system's balances.

For example, to reduce the incentive for fruitless wrangling and conflict between the branches and to encourage better cooperation, we have considered an amendment to allow presidents to name sitting members of Congress to their cabinets. Would it strengthen the executive's hand in dealing with Congress to have leading legislators on the president's team? Or would it weaken the president if he came to depend politically on these legislators in his administration?

Or if we replace the electoral college with a direct popular election for president, we will probably loosen the hold of the two-party system over national political life. Should we try somehow to offset that effect, perhaps by adopting some form of the team ticket, or channeling public funds for campaign financing through party organizations?

Should we consider the item veto as part of this package, to strengthen the president's hand in dealing with Congress? (The item veto is a device to allow the president to strike particular items from a bill that appropriates money for public programs. For example, if a bill provided money for improvements to rivers and harbors, and if the president believed that several of the projects in the bill were unnecessary or harmful, he might strike out those items before signing the bill.) The item veto is usually presented as a means of enabling presidents to prevent wasteful expenditures. But critics reply that the executive might use it in ways that actually increased expenditures, by threatening, for example, to veto a highway project in a member's district unless the member agreed to vote for an expensive new missile system. In any case, it seems clear that the item veto would strengthen the president's hand. It might therefore be useful as part of a package with other elements that might weaken the president's leverage over Congress.

We might also consider the legislative veto. For a half century, beginning in the early 1930s, Congress often qualified its grants of discretionary authority to the executive by providing that administrators could act, subject to the power of Congress to void the action by adopting a resolution of disapproval. The device enabled Congress to grant broad powers without losing control. It seemed like a useful development, well suited to an age when statutes could not give precise guidance to administrators without being ridiculously long, cumbersome and rigid.

Then, in 1983, the Supreme Court ruled that legislative vetos were unconstitutional. The Court insisted that the Constitution established only one procedure for enacting laws; once enacted, laws ought not to be subject to any further congressional modification, except by the usual procedures: repeal or statutory revision.

To some (including justices who wrote dissenting opinions), the Court's ruling seemed wooden-headed. It struck down a device that had enabled the constitutional system to accommodate to a modern economy. Others, however, applauded the restoration of government by law. Interest groups had been using the legislative veto to thwart the government's efforts. Sometimes it was possible for a single chamber, or even a single committee, to block the administration's action.

In the wake of the Court's decision, observers wondered which branch would benefit most from the ruling against the legislative veto. Would the executive gain strength by throwing off the threat of a legislative veto? Or would Congress now withhold powers it had given to the executive on condition of retaining an ultimate check?

Court rulings since 1983 have not fully resolved this issue. Sometimes the executive's powers (to impound funds, for example) have been blocked by courts, on grounds that Congress would not have given the power to impound without retaining the power to override. Further evidence that the legislative veto had not been completely abandoned came when President Bush used a similar tactic in agreeing to allow Congress to review his Central American policy in the fall of 1989 before sending the rest of the money Congress had appropriated for the contras in Nicaragua.

Thus, the legislative veto is in limbo. It might be added, in some variant, to a package of reforms intended to adjust the relations between the executive and Congress. If it were enshrined in a constitutional amendment, it would be beyond the power of the Supreme Court to end it. Obviously, the concerns of the Court in its 1983 ruling would be taken into account in framing such an amendment.

Changing the procedure for ratifying treaties is another reform that might become part of a package to readjust legislative-executive relations. Treaties now cannot take effect until the Senate votes its consent by a two-thirds majority. Some people believe that this special majority is too difficult to achieve and that presidents often act by executive agreement to evade the cumbersome process of ratifying treaties. The trouble with executive agreements is that the role of the Senate as a body of advice and consent is diminished.[1] If the Senate majority for ratifying treaties were reduced to three-fifths, or if treaties could be ratified by simple majorities of both houses of Congress, treaty-making might be restored to its traditional role in American diplomacy. In any thorough review of constitutional relationships between the legislative and executive branches, these issues ought probably to be included.

One of the basic concerns of this book, and generally of those who identify with the Committee on the Constitutional System, is the state of the party system. We have given consideration at several points to the argument that our political system suffers as we turn toward our third century as an independent nation in large part because we lack adequate means to link voters with one another, and the electorate with elected officials, and officials to one another. One way to strengthen these ties is to encourage candidates to run as part of a team, and to enable voters to support or oppose candidates as teams.

What effect would it have on our system of "separated institutions, sharing powers" if candidates for national office were forced to run as a team? Which institution would be strengthened: the presidency or Congress? It may seem obvious at first that it would strengthen the candidates for president, who seem to dominate current national campaigns so completely. But it might end up weakening the presidency. Candidates for Congress, seeing that the presidential campaign suddenly had such fateful significance for their own candidacies, might move to take control over the presidential nominating process in their own parties. They certainly could not afford to distance themselves from it, as they now often do.

Finally, consider the effect of lengthening the terms of members of the House to four years and making those terms coincide with the president's. Again, it is not entirely clear which branch, or which party, would be strengthened by this reform over the long run. If members of the House never ran alone, would they lose some of their insulation from the presidential race? If so, might they not be more willing to spend resources on their party's efforts at the presidential level?

The other effect of this reform is more certain: it would eliminate the mid-term "correction" (or at any rate reduce it substantially, even if we kept the six-year term for senators and continued to elect one-third of the Senate every two years). It would give us an executive and a House of Representatives, at least, fixed in place for four years, barring impeachment.

Concern about this prospect has led some people to insist that we should not extend House terms to four years without building in a safeguard. The possibility of calling special elections, to be held whenever the president or a majority of Congress believed they were necessary, would enable us to escape from deadlock, or to terminate an administration that had lost its ability to govern, without having to wait for the full four years to elapse.

PART FOUR

HOW TO PROCEED

11
The Agenda of Reform

Some of the changes outlined in this book could be accomplished, if they seemed desirable, by enacting new laws or changes in the rules by which political parties manage their affairs; others, as we have seen, would require constitutional amendments. Before proceeding to discuss the procedures for amending the Constitution, we need to say a word about these other processes.

Laws are made by procedures set forth in the Constitution and well-known to most Americans. To enact a law, both houses of Congress must pass the same version of a bill and the president must sign it. Or, if the president vetoes the bill, both houses must pass it again, over the president's veto, by two-thirds majorities. A law, once enacted, is subject to review by the courts if a party to a suit challenges its constitutionality.

The process for rule-making by the political parties is less familiar to most Americans. Normally a party's rules are made by its quadrennial national convention, after preparation by a specially appointed commission. For example, the shift toward reliance on primaries to select delegates to the Democratic National Convention came about after the 1968 party convention promised that "all Democratic voters" by 1972 would have a "full and timely opportunity to participate" in nominating the party's candidates for president and vice-president.[1] Pursuant to this resolution, the party chairman, Senator Fred Harris of Oklahoma, created a 28-member Commission on Party Structure and Delegate Selection, chaired by Senator George McGovern of South Dakota. The report of that commission, entitled "Mandate for Reform," was published in April, 1970, and became the blueprint for the selection of delegates for the next national convention.

To illustrate how this process might work for one of the reforms outlined in this book, let us take, as an example, the case of putting a ceiling on campaign expenditures. A party's national convention, held every four years, is its highest formal authority. The national committee, a much smaller body, conducts the party's business between national conventions. Ongoing, day-to-day management is performed by a staff headed by the national chairperson. One of the approaches to the reform of campaign spending, outlined in Chapter 7, was for a party to set ceilings on campaign expenditures by its nominees and then hope, or arrange, for the other party to follow suit. It might be accomplished by having a national convention adopt a resolution committing the party in principle to set such ceilings and calling on the chairman to establish a commission to develop rules to achieve this end. To implement such a resolution before the next elections, the convention could authorize the party's national committee to approve the commission's rules, pending their formal ratification by the ensuing national convention.

Reform by Constitutional Amendment

For reforms that would require a constitutional amendment, we need to consider how that process works. (Even those who are dubious about the need for any of the constitutional amendments outlined in this book may wish to think about alternative ways of doing it, in case a call for amendment suddenly gains momentum.)

Article V of the Constitution outlines *two* ways to amend the Constitution. The purpose of the remainder of this chapter is to provide materials for a debate between these two options. For purposes of discussion, we will use one of these constitutional options (the traditional method) as our resolution and use the rebuttal to represent a preference for the option that has not yet been tried.

The Existing Situation

The traditional method, outlined in Article V of the Constitution, provides that whenever a proposed amendment passes both houses of Congress by two-thirds majorities, it is sent to the states for ratification. (Note that the president is not formally involved in this process.) The amendment becomes part of the Constitution when ratified by the legislatures, or by conventions, in three-quarters (thirty-eight) of the states. Congress determines whether the states' ratification must be by the legislatures thereof or by conventions called specifically set up for that purpose.

Article V also provides an alternative route to amendment. Whenever the legislatures of two-thirds (thirty-four) of the states make application, Congress "shall call a convention for proposing amendments." Amendments proposed by such a convention are subject to the same ratification procedure: by three-quarters of the states, either by their legislatures or by state conventions, as determined by Congress.

By the express terms of Article V, no amendment to the Constitution may deprive a state, without its consent, of "its equal suffrage in the Senate." (The Constitution also protected the slave trade from interference by amendment before 1808.) Otherwise, the Constitution sets no limit on the content of potential amendments.

The Basic Proposal

RESOLVED: That we should continue to use the traditional method of amending the Constitution: adoption by two-thirds vote in both houses of Congress, then ratification by three-quarters of the states.

Discussion

If substantial opinion developed in the country that the existing system of government were no longer adequate, pressure would build for Congress to draft amendments to correct the faults. Attention would then turn to the question whether amendments could be fashioned that would produce improvements without dangerous side effects. If opinion began to coalesce around some leading alternatives, it would be up to Congress to draft the language of the proposed amendments. Presumably the judiciary committees of both houses would assume responsibility for preparing drafts, but other members, too—not to mention politicians, lobbyists, scholars and publicists outside of Congress—would make their own suggestions. The language hammered out by the committees would be subject to revision on the floors of both chambers. In the end, two-thirds majorities of both chambers would have to agree on common language.

The amendments thus proposed would proceed to the states. At this stage, Congress would have the authority, under Article V, to determine whether the legislatures of the states, or conventions elected especially for this purpose, would decide on ratification. Only once has Congress committed the ratification of constitutional amendments to conventions, rather than state legislatures. The exception was for the Twenty-first Amendment, which repealed the Eighteenth Amendment's prohibition of "the manufacture, sale, or transportation of intoxicating liquors." Congress knew that the temperance movement was strong in several state legislatures. The groundswell of popular demand for repeal was expected to meet less resistance in specially elected conventions than in state legislatures.

As soon as three-quarters of the states decided to ratify an amendment, the secretary of state would certify that the amendment was "valid, to all intents and purposes, as part of this Constitution."

The Alternative: A Modern Federal Convention

As for the alternative method of amending the Constitution—that is, by a special constitutional convention—Article V is vague on several important points. Among the unsettled issues are the following: Can Congress limit the agenda of the convention to the issues specified in the petitions? How will the delegates be chosen? Is anyone ineligible? Who sets the procedures for choosing delegates? How long is a state's petition for a constitutional convention valid? Can a state rescind its petition? Once a convention is called, can it set its own rules? Are its deliberations subject to review?

In an effort to settle these questions, Senator Orrin Hatch (Republican, Utah), in January, 1983, presented a bill that would have provided

- that if a state petitions Congress for a convention on a particular topic, its petition must be specific enough to determine whether there is a consensus among the petitioning states on the need for such a convention, but the petitions of different states on a given topic need not be framed in identical language;
- that petitions must be honored for seven years (whereafter they would have to be renewed in order to remain active), and that states have a right to rescind their petitions;
- that states have delegates equal in number to their presidential electors, but no member of Congress may be a delegate;
- that delegates be required to take an oath to comply with limitations on the convention's agenda set by Congress, pursuant to the states' petitions;
- that Congress could refuse to transmit proposed amendments to the states for ratification if they violated the mandate of the convention; and
- that proposed amendments be subject to judicial review. (The purpose of this last clause is to give the states recourse against the procedural determinations of Congress.)

Senator Hatch's bill, which did not pass, was based on the assumption that Congress has the power to call and regulate a limited convention if the states specifically request one. As Senator Hatch put it in 1979, "A constitutional convention, while clearly remaining a unique and separate element of the government—a new branch of government, so to speak—is subject to the same limitations and checks and balances as the other, permanent branches of the government."[2]

This assumption is disputed by many legislators and scholars. A leading scholarly authority on this subject, Professor Walter E. Dellinger, of the Duke University Law School, testified at the hearings on Senator Hatch's bill: "I am persuaded that any Article V convention was intended to be free of the control both of Congress and the state legislatures." The framers, said Dellinger, did not want to give either Congress or the state legislatures exclusive authority to propose amendments. As an alternative to the method of amendment that begins with Congress, they provided for a "convention free to determine the nature of the problem, free to define the subject matter and free to compromise the competing interests at stake in the process of drafting a corrective amendment." State legislatures may call for such a convention, Dellinger concluded, "but neither they nor Congress may control it."[3]

As it stands now, with the defeat of Senator Hatch's bill, there is no legislation on these points, and indeed, no consensus that legislation to control the agenda or outcome of an Article V convention would have any effect. Two things, however, do seem clear. First, Congress can forestall calling an Article V convention by acting itself on a subject that has aroused widespread public concern; and second, nothing that a convention proposes will become valid as part of the Constitution until three-quarters of the states ratify it.

Relevant Facts

☐ Principles enunciated in the founding documents:
From the Declaration of Independence:

We hold these truths to be self-evident: . . . that whenever any form of government becomes destructive of these ends [the rights to life, liberty and the pursuit of happiness, and to government by consent of the governed], it is the right of the people to alter or abolish it, and to institute a new government, laying its foundation on such principles, and organizing its powers in such form, as to them shall seem most likely to effect their safety and happiness. Prudence, indeed, will dictate that governments long established should not be changed for light and transient causes. . . . But when a long train of abuses and usurpations pursuing invariably the same object evinces a design to reduce them under absolute despotism, it is their right, it is their duty to throw off such government, and to provide new guards for their future safety.

From the Articles of Confederation, America's national constitution from 1781 until the ratification of the Constitution:

The Articles of Confederation shall be inviolably observed by every state, and the Union shall be perpetual; nor shall any alteration at any time hereafter be made in any of them, unless such alteration is agreed to in a Congress of the United States, and be afterward confirmed by the legislature of every state.

Article VI of the Constitution makes "this Constitution . . . the supreme law of the land," and it binds "the senators and representatives . . . and the members of the several state legislatures, and all the executive and judicial officers, both of the United States and of the several states . . . to support this Constitution. . . ." The Constitution, of course, includes Article V, which provides for amendments.

☐ Since 1789, over 5,000 bills proposing amendments to the Constitution have been introduced by members of Congress. Of these, only thirty-three received the necessary two-thirds vote of both houses of Congress and proceeded to the states for ratification. Twenty-six were adopted; the remaining seven failed to be ratified. Two of the seven were sent to the states in the package with the first ten amendments, those we now call the "Bill of Rights." They dealt with reapportionment of legislative districts and congressional pay raises. The most recent measure to pass in Congress but fail to be ratified by the states was the so-called "Equal Rights Amendment" (ERA), prohibiting discrimination on the grounds of sex.

Each of the existing twenty-six amendments was proposed by Congress, and all but one of them were ratified by the state legislatures. The repeal of prohibition, as noted above, was ratified by state conventions.

☐ Over the two centuries since 1789, states have submitted more than 300 petitions to Congress calling for an amending convention, most of them during the 20th century. The early ones tended to favor general conventions; more recently the petitions have sought conventions to consider specific amendments.

In this century, state petitions have sought the direct election of senators, repeal of prohibition, and a two-term limit on presidents. In each of these cases, Congress acted to preempt the convention, drafting amendments itself and sending them out to the states for ratification.

☐ Article V requires Congress to "call a convention for proposing amendments" whenever two-thirds of the states make application. There are now fifty states. Therefore, Congress must call a convention when thirty-four states ask for it.

As of 1984, thirty-two states had petitioned Congress to call a convention for the purpose of proposing an amendment that would require the federal government to adopt a balanced budget.

Arguments in Favor of This Proposal

1. Capability of Congress. If the Constitution needs to be amended, why not use the tried and true method? Congress is not only experienced in the ways of government and well positioned to assess proposals for change, but it is also a very sensitive barometer of public feeling. The Seventeenth Amendment, which changed the ground-rules for electing senators, was proposed by a Senate that had been elected under the old rules. Doesn't that show that Congress will respond to sufficient and persistent public pressure, even if the personal interests of its members are jeopardized?

2. Limiting Agenda. There is no way that an Article V convention could be confined to a single issue, like the balanced budget. As soon as such a convention gathered, the precedent of 1787 would take hold. That convention, too, was called with a limited agenda: to amend the Articles of Confederation. If Washington and Hamilton and Madison could move quickly and boldly beyond their mandate, why should modern framers hesitate?

The prevailing authority on this question is James Madison, "the father of the Constitution," and specifically his argument, in *The Federalist,* number 40, that the framers were "not only warranted but required," as the faithful servants of their country, to "exercise the liberty" of exceeding their credentials. If they violated "both their powers and their obligations in proposing a Constitution [rather than simply amending the Articles], this ought nevertheless to be embraced, if it can be calculated to accomplish the views and happiness of the people of America." No lawyerly quibbling could prevail against such a magisterial precedent.

3. Potential Dangers. A modern constitutional convention would be full of risk. Buffeted by the hot breath of popular passion, delegates might be driven to disrupt the framers' carefully crafted system of checks and balances, the protections that minorities enjoy, and perhaps even the Bill of Rights. It is one thing for an isolated, agrarian nation to send delegates to meet in secret to frame a constitution. It is quite another for a modern nation, which bears awesome responsibilities for world security and global economic prosperity, to present the spectacle of revamping its constitutional foundations. As Melvin Laird, former secretary of defense, has written, "The mere act of convening a constitutional convention would send tremors throughout all those economies that depend on the dollar; would undermine our neighbors' confidence in our constitutional integrity; and would weaken not only our economic stability but the stability of the free world."[4]

Arguments Against This Proposal

1. Capability of Congress. Normally Congress is a perfectly fit body to consider constitutional amendments. But the Convention of 1787 saw clearly that Congress ought not to have a veto over all amendments to the Constitution. From the beginning, the framers insisted on this point. The Virginia Plan established the concept of an amendable constitution, including the notion that "the assent of the national legislature ought not be required" for proposed amendments. In situations where Congress was itself part of the problem, the framers knew that it would be self-defeating to require Congress to assent to reforms.[5]

The wisdom of the framers was demonstrated in the drive to change the method of electing senators. By the end of the nineteenth century, the progressive movement had persuaded most Americans that state legislatures were not fit to choose senators, but incumbent senators bitterly resisted the change. They knuckled under only when they realized that the change would certainly come about by means of a convention if they continued to block the usual route.

Some of the proposals discussed in this book would face bitter opposition in Congress, whatever their merits. For example, setting four-year congressional terms coinciding with a president's term would mean that members of Congress would always be subject to the vicissitudes of presidential politics, never able to run for office when local issues were paramount. Many members would resist that change.

Congress consists of people who have won office by the existing rules. So long as the existing system works well, Congress is well qualified to operate it. But members of Congress cannot be expected to judge objectively the system that has elevated them to high office. Members of Congress are, for the most part, astute, sensitive and high-minded men and women, but they are not angels. We should not rule out, in advance, a method of constitutional amendment that deliberately provides a measure of leverage over Congress.

2. Limiting Agenda. The agenda and outcome of a modern constitutional convention would be controlled by public opinion. If the people wanted a constitutional amendment requiring a balanced budget, but no other changes, there would be tremendous popular pressure to limit the agenda to that purpose and severe censure for those who sought to broaden the scope.

The ultimate control would be the necessity of ratification. Any amendment, whether proposed by Congress or by a convention, would have to be ratified by three-quarters of the states. If a convention that was called to propose a balanced-budget amendment produced an amendment to ban abortion, it could not become part of the Constitution unless and until three-quarters of the states ratified it.

Furthermore, as Milton Eisenhower remarked, those who fear a convention may be underestimating the commitment of the American people to the basic principles of republican government. "I know of no reason," he said, "to expect that delegates to a convention would be any less responsible or committed to upholding our basic liberties than are members of Congress."[6]

3. Potential Dangers. Opponents of a modern constitutional convention often talk as if they were defending the handiwork of the framers of 1787 against modern vandals. Established elites in the United States and elsewhere in the world might indeed find a new American constitutional convention threatening to their privileges. But the American tradition of self-government demands that the people retain the ability to "alter or abolish" any form of government that disappoints their hopes for free government. The provision for a constitutional convention incorporates this hope into the body of the Constitution.

You Decide

☐ Is Congress able to assess objectively the need for constitutional reforms?

☐ Would a modern constitutional convention "open Pandora's box"? Would it invite general instability? Would it be liable to undermine basic liberties?

Appendix: Constitution of the United States

We the People of the United States, in Order to form a more perfect Union, establish Justice, insure domestic Tranquility, provide for the common defence, promote the general Welfare, and secure the Blessings of Liberty to ourselves and our Posterity, do ordain and establish this Constitution for the United States of America.

ARTICLE. I.

Section. 1. All legislative Powers herein granted shall be vested in a Congress of the United States, which shall consist of a Senate and House of Representatives.

Section. 2. The House of Representatives shall be composed of Members chosen every second Year by the People of the several States, and the Electors in each State shall have the Qualifications requisite for Electors of the most numerous Branch of the State Legislature.

No Person shall be a Representative who shall have not attained to the Age of twenty five Years, and been seven Years a Citizen of the United States, and who shall not, when elected, be an Inhabitant of that State in which he shall be chosen.

[Representatives and direct Taxes shall be apportioned among the several States which may be included within this Union, according to their respective Numbers, which shall be determined by adding the whole Number of free Persons, including those bound to Service for a Term of Years, and excluding Indians not taxed, three fifths of all other Persons.]*[1] The actual Enumeration shall be made within three

---

*All bracketed portions have been changed by later amendments. See Notes for the specific amendment containing the change.

Years after the first Meeting of the Congress of the United States, and within every subsequent Term of ten Years, in such Manner as they shall by Law direct. The number of Representatives shall not exceed one for every thirty Thousand, but each State shall have at Least one Representative; and until such enumeration shall be made, the State of New Hampshire shall be entitled to chuse three, Massachusetts eight, Rhode-Island and Providence Plantations one, Connecticut five, New-York six, New Jersey four, Pennsylvania eight, Delaware one, Maryland six, Virginia ten, North Carolina five, South Carolina five, and Georgia three.

When vacancies happen in the Representation from any State, the Executive Authority thereof shall issue Writs of Election to fill such Vacancies.

The House of Representatives shall chuse their Speaker and other Officers; and shall have the sole Power of Impeachment.

Section. 3. The Senate of the United States shall be composed of two Senators from each State, [chosen by the Legislature thereof,][2] for six Years; and each Senator shall have one Vote.

Immediately after they shall be assembled in Consequence of the first Election, they shall be divided as equally as may be into three Classes. The Seats of the Senators of the first Class shall be vacated at the Expiration of the second Year, of the second Class at the Expiration of the fourth Year, and of the third Class at the Expiration of the sixth Year, so that one third may be chosen every second Year; [and if Vacancies happened by Resignation, or otherwise, during the Recess of the Legislature of any State, the Executive thereof may make temporary Appointments until the next Meeting of the Legislature, which shall then fill such Vacancies.][3]

No Person shall be a Senator who shall not have attained to the Age of thirty Years, and been nine Years a Citizen of the United States, and who shall not, when elected, be an Inhabitant of that State for which he shall be chosen.

The Vice President of the United States shall be President of the Senate, but shall have no Vote, unless they be equally divided.

The Senate shall chuse their other Officers, and also a President pro tempore, in the Absence of the Vice President, or when he shall exercise the Office of the President of the United States.

The Senate shall have the sole Power to try all Impeachments. When sitting for that Purpose, they shall be on Oath or Affirmation. When the President of the United States is tried, the Chief Justice shall preside: And no Person shall be convicted without the Concurrence of two thirds of the Members present.

Judgment in Cases of Impeachment shall not extend further than to removal from Office, and disqualification to hold and enjoy any Office of honor, Trust or Profit under the United States: but the Party convicted shall nevertheless be liable and subject to Indictment, Trial, Judgment and Punishment, according to Law.

Section. 4. The Times, Places and Manner of holding Elections for Senators and Representatives, shall be prescribed in each State by the Legislature thereof; but the Congress may at any time by Law make or alter such Regulations, except as to the Places of chusing Senators.

The Congress shall assemble at least once in every Year, and such Meeting shall be [on the first Monday in December,][4] unless they shall by Law appoint a different Day.

Section. 5. Each House shall be the Judge of the Elections, Returns and Qualifications of its own Members, and a Majority of each shall constitute a Quorum to do Business; but a smaller Number may adjourn from day to day, and may be authorized to compel the Attendance of absent Members, in such Manner, and under such Penalties as each House may provide.

Each House may determine the Rules of its Proceedings, punish its Members for disorderly Behaviour, and, with the Concurrence of two thirds, expel a Member.

Each House shall keep a Journal of its Proceedings, and from time to time publish the same, excepting such Parts as may in their Judgment require Secrecy; and the Yeas and Nays of the Members of either House on any question shall, at the Desire of one fifth of those Present, be entered on the Journal.

Neither House, during the Session of Congress, shall without the Consent of the other, adjourn for more than three days, nor to any other Place than that in which the two Houses shall be sitting.

Section. 6. The Senators and Representatives shall receive a Compensation for their Services, to be ascertained by Law, and paid out of the Treasury of the United States. They shall in all Cases, except Treason, Felony and Breach of the Peace, be privileged from Arrest during their Attendance at the Session of their respective Houses, and in going to and returning from the same; and for any Speech or Debate in either House, they shall not be questioned in any other Place.

No Senator or Representative shall, during the time for which he was elected, be appointed to any civil Office under the Authority of the United States, which shall have been created, or the Emoluments whereof shall have been encreased during such time; and no Person holding any Office under the United States, shall be a Member of either House during his Continuance in Office.

Section. 7. All Bills for raising Revenue shall originate in the House of Representatives; but the Senate may propose or concur with Amendments as on other Bills.

Every Bill which shall have passed the House of Representatives and the Senate, shall, before it becomes a Law, be presented to the President of the United States; If he approve he shall sign it, but if not he shall return it, with his Objections to that House in which it shall have originated, who shall enter the Objections at large on their Journal, and proceed to reconsider it. If after such Reconsideration two thirds of that House shall agree to pass the Bill, it shall be sent, together with the Objections, to the other House, by which it shall likewise be reconsidered, and if approved by two thirds of that House, it shall become a Law. But in all such Cases the Votes of both Houses shall be determined by yeas and Nays and the Names of the Persons voting for and against the Bill shall be entered on the Journal of each House respectively. If any Bill shall not be returned by the President within ten Days (Sundays excepted) after it shall have been presented to him, the Same shall be a Law, in like Manner as if he had signed it, unless the Congress by their Adjournment prevent its Return, in which Case it shall not be a Law.

Every Order, Resolution, or Vote to which the Concurrence of the Senate and House of Representatives may be necessary (except on a question of Adjournment) shall be presented to the President of the United States; and before the Same shall take Effect, shall be approved by him, or being disapproved by him, shall be repassed by two thirds of the Senate and House of Representatives, according to the Rules and Limitations prescribed in the Case of a Bill.

Section. 8. The Congress shall have Power To lay and collect Taxes, Duties, Imposts and Excises, to pay the Debts and provide for the common Defence and general Welfare of the United States; but all Duties, Imposts and Excises shall be uniform throughout the United States;

To borrow Money on the credit of the United States;

To regulate Commerce with foreign Nations, and among the several States, and with the Indian Tribes;

To establish an uniform Rule of Naturalization, and uniform Laws on the subject of Bankruptcies throughout the United States;

To coin Money, regulate the Value thereof, and of foreign Coin, and fix the Standard of Weights and Measures;

To provide for the Punishment of counterfeiting the Securities and current Coin of the United States;

To establish Post Offices and post Roads;

To promote the Progress of Science and useful Arts, by securing for limited Times to Authors and Inventors the exclusive Right to their respective Writings and Discoveries;

To constitute Tribunals inferior to the supreme Court;

To define and punish Piracies and Felonies committed on the high Seas, and Offenses against the Law of Nations;

To declare War, grant Letters of Marque and Reprisal, and make Rules concerning Captures on Land and Water;

To raise and support Armies, but no Appropriation of Money to that Use shall be for a longer Term than two Years;

To provide and maintain a Navy;

To make Rules for the Government and Regulation of the land and naval Forces;

To provide for calling forth the Militia to execute the Laws of the Union, suppress Insurrections and repel Invasions;

To provide for organizing, arming, and disciplining, the Militia, and for governing such Part of them as may be employed in the Service of the United States, reserving to the States respectively, the Appointment of the Officers, and the Authority of training the Militia according to the discipline prescribed by Congress;

To exercise exclusive Legislation in all Cases whatsoever, over such District (not exceeding ten Miles square) as may, by Cession of particular States, and the Acceptance of Congress, become the Seat of the Government of the United States, and to exercise the Authority over all Places purchased by the Consent of the Legislature of the State in which the Same shall be, for the Erection of Forts, Magazines, Arsenals, dock-Yards and other needful Buildings;—And

To make all Laws which shall be necessary and proper for carrying into Execution the foregoing Powers, and all other Powers vested by this Constitution in the Government of the United States, or in any Department or Officer thereof.

Section. 9. The Migration or Importation of such Persons as any of the States now existing shall think proper to admit, shall not be prohibited by the Congress prior to the Year one thousand eight hundred and eight, but a Tax or duty may be imposed on such Importation, not exceeding ten dollars for each Person.

The Privilege of the Writ of Habeas Corpus shall not be suspended, unless when in Cases of Rebellion or Invasion the public Safety may require it.

No Bill of Attainder or ex post facto Law shall be passed.

[No Capitation, or other direct, Tax shall be laid, unless in Proportion to the Census or Enumeration herein before directed to be taken.][5]

No Tax or Duty shall be laid on Articles exported from any State.

No Preference shall be given by any Regulation of Commerce or Revenue to the Ports of one State over those of another: nor shall Vessels bound to, or from, one State, be obliged to enter, clear, or pay Duties in another.

No Money shall be drawn from the Treasury, but in Consequence of Appropriations made by Law; and a regular Statement and Account of the Receipts and Expenditures of all public Money shall be published from time to time.

No Title of Nobility shall be granted by the United States: And no Person holding any Office of Profit or Trust under them, shall without the Consent of the Congress, accept of any present, Emolument, Office or Title, of any kind whatever, from any King, Prince, or foreign State.

Section. 10. No State shall enter into any Treaty, Alliance, or Confederation; grant Letters of Marque and Reprisal; coin Money; emit Bills of Credit; make any Thing but gold and silver Coin a Tender in Payment of Debts; pass any Bill of Attainder, ex post facto Law, or Law impairing the Obligation of Contracts, or grant any Title of Nobility.

No State shall, without the Consent of the Congress, lay any Imposts or Duties on Imports or Exports, except what may be absolutely necessary for executing it's inspection Laws: and the net Produce of all Duties and Imposts, laid by any State on Imports or Exports, shall be for the Use of the Treasury of the United States; and all such Laws shall be subject to the Revision and Controul of the Congress.

No State shall, without the Consent of the Congress, lay any Duty of Tonnage, keep Troops, or Ships of War in time of Peace, enter into any Agreement or Compact with another State, or with a foreign Power, or engage in War, unless actually invaded, or in such imminent Danger as will not admit of delay.

ARTICLE. II.

Section. 1. The executive Power shall be vested in a President of the United States of America. He shall hold his Office during the Term of four Years, and, together with the Vice President, chosen for the same Term, be elected, as follows

Each State shall appoint, in such Manner as the Legislature thereof may direct, a Number of Electors, equal to the whole Number of Senators and Representatives to which the State may be entitled in the Congress: but no Senator or Representative, or Person holding an Office of Trust or Profit under the United States, shall be appointed an Elector.

[The Electors shall meet in their respective States, and vote by Ballot for two Persons, of whom one at least shall not be an Inhabitant of the same State with themselves. And they shall make a List of all the Persons voted for, and the Number of Votes for each; which List they shall sign and certify, and transmit sealed to the Seat of the Government of the United States, directed to the President of the Senate. The President of the Senate shall, in the Presence of the Senate and House of Representatives, open all the Certificates, and the Votes shall then be counted. The Person having the greatest Number of Votes shall be the President, if such Number be a Majority of the whole Number of Electors appointed; and if there be more than one who have such Majority, and have an equal Number of Votes, then the House of Representatives shall immediately chuse by Ballot one of them for President; and if no Person have a Majority, then from the five highest on the List the said House shall in like Manner chuse the President. But in chusing the President, the Votes shall be taken by the States, the Representation from each State having one Vote; A quorum for this Purpose shall consist of a Member or Members from two thirds of the States, and a Majority of all the States shall be necessary to a Choice. In every Case, after the Choice of the President, the Person having the greatest Number of Votes of the Electors shall be the Vice President. But if there should remain two or more who have equal Votes, the Senate shall chuse from them by Ballot the Vice President.][6]

The Congress may determine the Time of chusing the Electors, and the Day on which they shall give their Votes; which Day shall be the same throughout the United States.

No Person except a natural born Citizen, or a Citizen of the United States, at the time of the Adoption of this Constitution, shall be eligible to the Office of the President; neither shall any person be eligible to that Office who shall not have attained to the Age of thirty five Years, and been fourteen Years a Resident within the United States.

[In Case of the Removal of the President from Office or of his Death, Resignation, or Inability to discharge the Powers and Duties of the said Office, the Same shall devolve on the Vice President, and the Congress may by Law provide for the Case of Removal, Death, Resignation or Inability, both of the President and Vice President, declaring what Officer shall then act as President, and such Officer shall act accordingly, until the Disability be removed, or a President shall be elected.][7]

The President shall, at stated Times, receive for his Services, a Compensation, which shall neither be increased nor diminished during the Period for which he shall have been elected, and he shall not receive within that Period any other Emolument from the United States, or any of them.

Before he enter on the Execution of his Office, he shall take the following Oath or Affirmation:—"I do solemnly swear (or affirm) that I will faithfully execute the Office of President of the United States, and will to the best of my Ability, preserve, protect and defend the Constitution of the United States."

Section. 2. The President shall be Commander in Chief of the Army and Navy of the United States, and the Militia of the several States, when called into the actual Service of the United States; he may require the Opinion, in writing, of the principal Officer in each of the executive Departments, upon any Subject relating to the Duties of their respective Offices, and he shall have Power to grant Reprieves and Pardons for Offenses against the United States, except in Cases of Impeachment.

He shall have Power, by and with the Advice and Consent of the Senate, to make Treaties, provided two thirds of the Senators present concur; and he shall nominate, and by and with the Advice and Consent of the Senate, shall appoint Ambassadors, other pubic Ministers and Consuls, Judges of the supreme Court, and all other Officers of the United States, whose Appointments are not herein otherwise provided for, and which shall be established by Law: but the Congress may by Law vest the Appointment of such inferior Officers, as they think proper, in the President alone, in the Courts of Law, or in the Heads of Departments.

The President shall have Power to fill up all Vacancies that may happen during the Recess of the Senate, by granting Commissions which shall expire at the End of their next Session.

Section. 3. He shall from time to time give to the Congress Information of the State of the Union, and recommend to their Consideration such Measures as he shall judge necessary and expedient; he may, on extraordinary Occasions, convene both Houses, or either of them, and in Case of Disagreement between them, with Respect to the Time of Adjournment, he may adjourn them to such Time as he shall think proper; he shall receive Ambassadors and other public Ministers; he shall take Care that the Laws be faithfully executed, and shall Commission all the Officers of the United States.

Section. 4. The President, Vice President and all civil Officers from the United States, shall be removed from Office on Impeachment for, and Conviction of, Treason, Bribery, or other high Crimes and Misdemeanors.

ARTICLE. III.

Section. 1. The judicial Power of the United States, shall be vested in one supreme Court, and in such inferior Courts as the Congress may from time to time ordain and establish. The Judges, both of the supreme and inferior Courts, shall hold their Offices during good Behaviour, and shall, at stated Times, receive for their Services, a Compensation, which shall not be diminished during their Continuance in Office.

Section. 2. The judicial Power shall extend to all Cases, in Law and Equity, arising under this Constitution, the Laws of the United States, and Treaties made, or which shall be made, under their Authority;—to all Cases affecting Ambassadors, other public Ministers and Consuls;—to all Cases of admiralty and maritime Jurisdiction;—to Controversies to which the United States shall be a Party;—to Controversies between two or more States;—[between a State and Citizens of another State;]8—between Citizens of different States;—between Citizens of the same State claiming Lands under Grants of different States[, and between a State, or the Citizens thereof, and foreign States, Citizens or Subjects].9

In all Cases affecting Ambassadors, other public Ministers and Consuls, and those in which a State shall be Party, the supreme Court shall have original Jurisdiction. In all the other Cases before mentioned, the supreme Court shall have appellate Jurisdiction, both as to Law and Fact, with such Exceptions, and under such Regulations as the Congress shall make.

The Trial of all Crimes, except in Cases of Impeachment, shall be by Jury; and such Trial shall be held in the State where the said Crimes shall have been committed; but when not committed within any State, the Trial shall be at such Place or Places as the Congress may by Law have directed.

Section. 3. Treason against the United States, shall consist only in levying War against them, or in adhering to their Enemies, giving them Aid and Comfort. No Person shall be convicted of Treason unless on the Testimony of two Witnesses to the same overt Act, or on Confession in open Court.

The Congress shall have Power to declare the Punishment of Treason, but no Attainder of Treason shall work Corruption of Blood, or Forfeiture except during the Life of the Person attained.

ARTICLE. IV.

Section. 1. Full Faith and Credit shall be given in each State to the public Acts, Records, and judicial Proceedings of every other State; And the Congress may by general Laws prescribe the Manner in which such Acts, Records and Proceedings shall be proved, and the Effect thereof.

Section. 2. The Citizens of each State shall be entitled to all Privileges and Immunities of Citizens in the several States.

A Person charged in any State with Treason, Felony, or other Crime, who shall flee from Justice, and be found in another State, shall on Demand of the executive Authority of the State from which he fled, be delivered up, to be removed to the State having Jurisdiction of the Crime.

[No Person held to Service or Labour in one State, under the Laws thereof, escaping into another, shall in Consequence of any Law or Regulation therein, be discharged from such Service or Labour, but shall be delivered up on Claim of the Party to whom such Service or Labour may be due.][10]

Section. 3. New States may be admitted by the Congress into this Union; but no new State shall be formed or erected within the Jurisdiction of any other State; nor any State be formed by the Junction of two or more States, or Parts of States, without the Consent of the Legislatures of the States concerned as well as the Congress.

The Congress shall have Power to dispose of and make all needful Rules and Regulations respecting the Territory or other Property belonging to the United States; and nothing in this Constitution shall be so construed as to Prejudice any Claims of the United States, or any particular State.

Section. 4. The United States shall guarantee to every State in this Union a Republican Form of Government, and shall protect each of them against Invasion; and on Application of the Legislature, or of the Executive (when the Legislature cannot be convened) against domestic Violence.

ARTICLE. V.

The Congress, whenever two thirds of both Houses shall deem it necessary, shall propose Amendments to this Constitution, or on the Application of the Legislatures of two thirds of the several States, shall call a Convention for proposing Amendments, which, in either Case, shall be valid to all Intents and Purposes, as Part of this Constitution, when ratified by the Legislatures of three fourths of the several States, or by Conventions in three fourths thereof, as the one or the other Mode of Ratification may be proposed by the Congress; Provided that no Amendment which may be made prior to the Year One thousand eight hundred and eight shall in any Manner affect the first and fourth Clauses in the Ninth Section of the first Article; and that no State, without its Consent, shall be deprived of its equal Suffrage in the Senate.

ARTICLE. VI.

All Debts contracted and Engagements entered into, before the Adoption of this Constitution, shall be as valid against the United States under this Constitution, as under the Confederation.

This Constitution, and the Laws of the United States which shall be made in Pursuance thereof; and all Treaties made, or which shall be made, under the Authority of the United States, shall be the supreme Law of the Land; and the Judges in every State shall be bound thereby, any Thing in the Constitution or Laws of any State to the Contrary notwithstanding.

The Senators and Representatives before mentioned, and the Members of the several State Legislatures, and all executive and judicial Officers, both of the United States and of the several States, shall be bound by Oath or Affirmation, to support this Constitution; but no religious Test shall ever be required as a Qualification to any Office or public Trust under the United States.

ARTICLE. VII.

The Ratification of the Conventions of nine States shall be sufficient for the Establishment of this Constitution between the States so ratifying the Same.

AMENDMENT I. (1791)

Congress shall make no law respecting an establishment of religion, or prohibiting the free exercise thereof; or abridging the freedom of speech, or the press, or the right of the people peaceably to assemble, and to petition the Government for a redress of grievances.

AMENDMENT II. (1791)

A well regulated Militia, being necessary to the security of a free State, the right of the people to keep and bear Arms, shall not be infringed.

AMENDMENT III. (1791)

No Soldier shall, in time of peace be quartered in any house, without the consent of the Owner, nor in time of war, but in a manner to be prescribed by law.

AMENDMENT IV. (1791)

The right of the people to be secure in their persons, houses, papers, and effects, against unreasonable searches and seizures, shall not be violated and no Warrants shall issue, but upon probable cause, supported by Oath or affirmation, and particularly describing the place to be searched, and the persons or things to be seized.

AMENDMENT V. (1791)

No person shall be held to answer for a capital, or otherwise infamous crime, unless on a presentment or indictment of a Grand Jury, except in cases arising in the land or naval forces, or in the Militia, when in actual service in time of War or public danger; nor shall any person be subject for the same offence to be twice put in jeopardy of life or limb, nor shall be compelled in any criminal case to be a witness against himself, nor be deprived of life, liberty, or property, without due process of law; nor shall private property be taken for public use without just compensation.

AMENDMENT VI. (1791)

In all criminal prosecutions, the accused shall enjoy the right to a speedy and public trial, by an impartial jury of the State and district wherein the crime shall have been committed; which district shall have been previously ascertained by law, and to be informed of the nature and cause of the accusation; to be confronted with the witnesses against him; to have compulsory process for obtaining witness in his favor, and to have the assistance of counsel for his defence.

AMENDMENT VII. (1791)

In Suits at common law, where the value in controversy shall exceed twenty dollars, the right of trial by jury shall be preserved, and no fact tried by a jury shall be otherwise re-examined in any Court of the United States, than according to the rules of the common law.

AMENDMENT VIII. (1791)

Excessive bail shall not be required, nor excessive fines imposed, nor cruel and unusual punishments inflicted.

AMENDMENT IX. (1791)

The enumeration in the Constitution of certain rights shall not be construed to deny or disparage others retained by the people.

AMENDMENT X. (1791)

The powers not delegated to the United States by the Constitution, nor prohibited by it to the States, are reserved to the States respectively, or to the people.

AMENDMENT XI. (1795)

The Judicial power of the United States shall not be construed to extend to any suit in law or equity, commenced or prosecuted against one of the United States by Citizens of another State, or by Citizens or Subjects of any Foreign State.

AMENDMENT XII. (1804)

The Electors shall meet in their respective states, and vote by ballot for President and Vice-President, one of whom, at least, shall not be an inhabitant of the same state with themselves; they shall name in their ballots the person voted for as President, and in distinct ballots the person voted for as Vice-President, and they shall make distinct lists of all persons voted for as President, and of all persons voted for as Vice-President, and of the number of votes for each, which lists they shall sign and certify, and transmit sealed to the seat of the government of the United States, directed to the President of the Senate;—The President of the Senate shall, in the presence of the Senate and House of Representatives, open all the certificates and the votes shall then be counted;—The person having the greatest number of votes for President, shall be the President, if such number be a majority of the whole number of Electors appointed; and if no person have such majority, then from the persons having the highest numbers not exceeding three on the list of those voted for as President, the House of Representatives shall choose immediately, by ballot, the President. But in choosing the President, the votes shall be taken by states, the representation from each state having one vote; a quorum for this purpose shall consist of a member or members from two-thirds of the states, and a majority of all the states shall be necessary to a choice. [And if the House of Representatives shall not choose a President whenever the right of choice shall devolve upon them, before the fourth day of March next following, then the Vice-President shall act as President, as in the case of the death or other constitutional disability of the President—][11]The person having the greatest number of votes as Vice-President, shall be the Vice-President, if such number be a majority of the whole number of Electors appointed, and if no person have a majority, then from the two highest numbers on the list, the Senate shall choose the Vice-President; a quorum for the purpose shall consist of two-thirds of the whole number of Senators, and a majority of the whole number shall be necessary to a choice. But no person constitutionally ineligible to the office of President shall be eligible to that of Vice-President of the United States.

AMENDMENT XIII. (1865)

Section 1. Neither slavery nor involuntary servitude, except as a punishment for crime whereof the party shall have been duly convicted, shall exist within the United States, or any place subject to their jurisdiction.

Section 2. Congress shall have power to enforce this article by appropriate legislation.

AMENDMENT XIV. (1868)

Section 1. All persons born or naturalized in the United States and subject to the jurisdiction thereof, are citizens of the United States and of the State wherein they reside. No State shall make or enforce any law which shall abridge the privileges or immunities of citizens of the United States; nor shall any State deprive any person of life, liberty or property, without due process of law; nor deny to any person within its jurisdiction the equal protection of the laws.

Section 2. Representatives shall be apportioned among the several States according to their respective numbers, counting the whole number of persons in each State, excluding Indians not taxed. But when the right to vote at any election for the choice of electors for President and Vice President of the United States, Representatives in Congress, the Executive and Judicial officers of a State, or the members of the Legislature thereof, is denied to any of the male inhabitants of such State, being twenty-one years of age, and citizens of the United States, or in any way abridged, except for participation in rebellion, or other crime, the basis for representation therein shall be reduced in the proportion which the number of such male citizens shall bear to the whole number of male citizens twenty-one years of age in such State.

Section 3. No person shall be a Senator or Representative in Congress, or elector of President and Vice-President, or hold any office, civil or military, under the United States, or under any State, who, having previously taken an oath, as a member of Congress, or as an officer of the United States, or as a member of any State legislature, or as an executive or judicial officer of any State, to support the Constitution of the United States, shall have engaged in insurrection or rebellion against the same, or given aid or comfort to the enemies thereof. But Congress may by a vote of two-thirds of each House, remove such disability.

Section 4. The validity of the public debt of the United States, authorized by law, including debts incurred for payment of pensions and bounties for services in suppressing insurrection or rebellion shall not be questioned. But neither the United States nor any State shall assume or pay any debt or obligation incurred in aid of insurrection or rebellion against the United States, or any claim for the loss or emancipation of any slave; but all such debts, obligations and claims shall be held illegal and void.

Section 5. The Congress shall have power to enforce, by appropriate legislation, the provisions of this article.

AMENDMENT XV. (1870)

Section 1. The right of citizens of the United States to vote shall not be denied or abridged by the United States or by any State on account of race, color, or previous condition of servitude.

Section 2. The Congress shall have power to enforce this article by appropriate legislation.

AMENDMENT XVI. (1913)

The Congress shall have power to lay and collect taxes on incomes, from whatever source derived, without apportionment among the several States, and without regard to any census or enumeration.

AMENDMENT XVII. (1913)

The Senate of the United States shall be composed of two Senators from each State, elected by the people thereof, for six years; and each Senator shall have one vote. The electors in each State shall have the qualifications requisite for electors of the most numerous branch of the State legislatures.

When vacancies happen in the representation of any State in the Senate, the executive authority of such State shall issue writs of election to fill such vacancies: *Provided,* That the legislature of any State may empower the executive thereof to make temporary appointments until the people fill the vacancies by election as the legislature may direct.

This amendment shall not be so construed as to affect the election or term of any Senator chosen before it becomes valid as part of the Constitution.

AMENDMENT XVIII. (1919)

Section 1. After one year from the ratification of this article the manufacture, sale, or transportation of intoxicating liquors within, the importation thereof into, or the exportation thereof from the United States and all territory subject to the jurisdiction thereof for beverage purposes is hereby prohibited.

Section 2. The Congress and the several States shall have concurrent power to enforce this article by appropriate legislation.

Section 3. This article shall be inoperative unless it shall have been ratified as an amendment to the Constitution by the legislatures of the several States, as provided in the Constitution, within seven years from the date of the submission hereof to the States by the Congress.

AMENDMENT XIX. (1920)

The right of citizens of the United States to vote shall not be denied or abridged by the United States or by any State on account of sex.

Congress shall have power to enforce this article by appropriate legislation.

AMENDMENT XX. (1933)

Section 1. The terms of the President and Vice President shall end at noon on the 20th day of January, and the terms of Senators and Representatives at noon on the 3d day of January, of the years in which such terms would have ended if this article had not been ratified; and the terms of their successors shall then begin.

Section 2. The Congress shall assemble at least once in every year, and such meeting shall begin at noon on the 3d day of January, unless they shall by law appoint a different day.

Section 3. If, at the time fixed for the beginning of the term of the President, the President elect shall have died, the Vice President elect shall become President. If a President shall not have been chosen before the time fixed for the beginning of his term, or if the President elect shall have failed to qualify, then the Vice President elect shall act as President until a President shall have qualified; and the Congress may by law provide for the case wherein neither a President elect nor a Vice President elect shall have qualified, declaring who shall then act as President, or the manner in which one who is to act shall be selected, and such person shall act accordingly until a President or Vice President shall have qualified.

Section 4. The Congress may by law provide for the case of the death of any of the persons from whom the House of Representatives may choose a President whenever the right of choice shall have devolved upon them, and for the case of the death of any of the persons from whom the Senate may choose a Vice President whenever the right of choice shall have devolved upon them.

Section 5. Sections 1 and 2 shall take effect on the 15th day of October following the ratification of this article.

Section 6. This article shall be inoperative unless it shall have been ratified as an amendment to the Constitution by the legislatures of three-fourths of the several States within seven years from the date of its submission.

AMENDMENT XXI. (1933)

Section 1. The eighteenth article of amendment to the Constitution of the United States is hereby repealed.

Section 2. The transportation or importation into any State, Territory, or possession of the United States for delivery or use therein of intoxicating liquors, in violation of the laws thereof, is hereby prohibited.

Section 3. This article shall be inoperative unless it shall have been ratified as an amendment to the Constitution by conventions of the several States, as provided in the Constitution, within seven years from the date of the submission hereof to the States by the Congress.

AMENDMENT XXII. (1951)

Section 1. No person shall be elected to the office of the President more than twice, and no person who has held office of President, or acted as President, for more than two years of a term to which some other person was elected President shall be elected to the office of the President more than once. But this Article shall not apply to any person holding the office of President when this Article was proposed by the Congress, and shall not prevent any person who may be holding the office of President, or acting as President, during the term within which this Article becomes operative from holding the office of President or acting as President during the remainder of such term.

Section 2. The article shall be inoperative unless it shall have been ratified as an amendment to the Constitution by the legislatures of three-fourth of the several States within seven years from the date of its submission to the States by the Congress.

AMENDMENT XXIII. (1961)

Section 1. The District constituting the seat of Government of the United States shall appoint in such manner as the Congress may direct:
A number of electors of President and Vice President equal to the whole number of Senators and Representatives in Congress to which the District would be entitled if it were a State, but in no event more than the least populous State; they shall be in addition to those appointed by the States, but they shall be considered, for the purposes of the election of President and Vice President, to be electors appointed by a State; and they shall meet in the District and perform such duties as provided by the twelfth article of amendment.

Section 2. The Congress shall have power to enforce this article by appropriate legislation.

AMENDMENT XXIV. (1964)

Section 1. The right of citizens of the United States to vote in any primary or other election for President or Vice President, for electors for President or Vice President, or for Senator or Representative in Congress, shall not be denied or abridged by the United States or any State by reason of failure to pay any poll tax or other tax.

Section 2. The Congress shall have power to enforce this article by appropriate legislation.

AMENDMENT XXV. (1967)

Section 1. In case of the removal of the President from office or of his death or resignation, the Vice President shall become President.

Section 2. Whenever there is a vacancy in the office of the Vice President, the President shall nominate a Vice President who shall take office upon confirmation by a majority vote of both Houses of Congress.

Section 3. Whenever the President transmits to the President pro tempore of the Senate and the Speaker of the House of Representatives his written declaration that he is unable to discharge the powers and duties of his office, and until he transmits to them a written declaration to the contrary, such powers and duties shall be discharged by the Vice President as Acting President.

Section 4. Whenever the Vice President and a majority of either the principal officers of the executive departments or of such other body as Congress may by law provide, transmit to the President pro tempore of the Senate and the Speaker of the House of Representatives their written declaration that the President is unable to discharge the powers and duties of his office, the Vice President shall immediately assume the powers and duties of the office as Acting President.

Thereafter, when the President transmits to the President pro tempore of the Senate and the Speaker of the House of Representatives his written declaration that no inability exists, he shall resume the powers and duties of his office unless the Vice President and a majority of either the principal officers of the executive department or of such other body as Congress may by law provide, transmit within four days to the President pro tempore of the Senate and the Speaker of the House of Representatives their written declaration that the President is unable to discharge the powers and duties of his office. Thereupon Congress shall decide the issue, assembling within forty-eight hours for that purpose if not in session. If the Congress, within twenty-one days after receipt of the latter written declaration, or if Congress is not in session, within twenty-one days after Congress is required to assemble, determines by two-thirds vote of both Houses that the President is unable to discharge the powers and duties of his office, the Vice President shall continue to discharge the same as Acting President; otherwise, the President shall resume the powers and duties of his office.

AMENDMENT XXVI. (1971)

Section 1. The right of citizens of the United States, who are eighteen years of age or older, to vote shall not be denied or abridged by the United States or by any State on account of age.

Section 2. The Congress shall have power to enforce this article by appropriate legislation.

Notes

CHAPTER 1

1. *The Federalist,* number 85.
2. Printed in Donald L. Robinson, editor, *Reforming American Government* (Westview Press, 1985), pp. 59–60.

CHAPTER 2

1. Stephen Hess, *The Presidential Campaign,* third edition (Brookings, 1988), pp. 47–49.
2. Nancy Landon Kassebaum, "Statement on Campaign Finance," in Donald L. Robinson, editor, *Reforming American Government* (Westview Press, 1985), pp. 30–32.
3. Everett Carll Ladd, *The American Polity,* second edition (W. W. Norton, 1987), p. 450.
4. *Ibid.,* p. 450.
5. Curtis Gans, "Non-Voter Study '78–'79," a report of the Committee for the Study of the American Electorate (December, 1978), p. 6; quoted by Ladd, *The American Polity,* p. 455. Raymond Wolfinger and Steven Rosenstone conclude that if the government were to take responsibility for registering all eligible voters, the national turnout would increase by about 9 percent. See *Who Votes?* (Yale University Press, 1980), p. 88. For a thoughtful survey of the turnout problem, see Debra Duff and William Woodwell, Jr., "An Absence of Ballots," in *National Voter* (magazine of the League of Women Voters), April/May, 1989, pp. 4–9.
6. We must view these statistics with some skepticism. States sometimes reported results that showed vote totals that were greater than the number of eligible voters. Even so, it seems clear that turnout rates were substantially higher then than they are now.
7. Martin P. Wattenberg concludes: "Ticket-splitting has assumed massive proportions compared to the rate just two decades ago, and only a small minority of the electorate now believes that one should vote strictly on the basis of party labels." See *The Decline of American Political Parties, 1952–1980* (Harvard University Press, 1984), p. 23.

8. Austin Ranney, *Channels of Power* (Basic Books, 1983). He persuasively argues that television has affected the conduct of American government less than we sometimes think, but the most significant effects have been in the electoral arena.

9. Wattenberg, *Decline of Parties,* p. 23.

10. James L. Sundquist, "Strengthening the National Parties," in A. James Reichley, editor, *Elections American Style* (Brookings, 1987), pp. 214–216.

11. Lloyd N. Cutler, "Party Government Under the Constitution," reprinted in Robinson, *Reforming American Government,* pp. 100–102.

12. Wattenberg, *Decline of Parties,* pp. 16 and 22.

CHAPTER 3

1. Michael Harrington, *The Other America: Poverty in the United States* (Penguin Books, 1981).

2. Robert Heilbroner, *The Future As History* (Harper & Row, 1960).

3. Tom Wicker, *New York Times,* July 19, 1988, p. A31.

4. Emma Rothschild, in *New York Review of Books,* June 30, 1988, p. 51. Generally, see Lester Thurow, "The Moral Equivalent of Defeat," *Foreign Policy* (Spring 1981), printed in Donald L. Robinson, editor, *Reforming American Government* (Westview Press, 1985), 33–38.

5. Rothschild, *op. cit.,* p. 52.

6. *Ibid.,* p. 35, n. 19.

7. From 1870 until 1930, excepting a two-year period during World War I, the federal government's total expenditures as a proportion of the GNP averaged less than 5 percent; since 1960, they have been over 20 percent. James Q. Wilson, *American Government,* fourth edition (D. C. Heath and Co., 1989), p. 450.

8. James M. Buchanan and Richard E. Wagner, *Democracy in Deficit* (Academic Press, 1977), esp. ch. 2.

9. The president added, "For all their talk about the deficit, the liberal Democrats in Congress have not been able to control their big spending ways." The text of Reagan's address is in *Weekly Compilation of Presidential Documents* 1986, p. 1287.

10. Congressional Democrats were not alone in believing that the answer had to come from the revenue side. In 1986, the administration's former budget director, David Stockman, concluded his blockbuster book, *The Triumph of Politics,* with this plea: "It is still not too late for the nation's most imposing politician [Reagan] to join with other politicians and do what together they must: Trim a little more spending where the democratic consensus will permit it, and raise a lot of new taxes to pay for the government the nation has decided it wants." (Harper & Row, 1986), p. 394. In this connection, it is perhaps worth noting that the United States in 1984 stood seventeenth in a list of nineteen constitutional democracies, in terms of total tax revenues as a percentage of gross national product. Sweden topped the list with 50.5 percent, the U.K. 38.5 percent, West Germany 37.7 percent, Canada 33.7

percent, and the U.S. 29.0 percent. Only Spain (28.4 percent) and Japan (27.4 percent) ranked lower. See *Statistical Abstract of the United States,* 1987, p. 828.

11. In a typical finding, the Gallup poll in 1985 showed that 58 percent regarded the deficit as a "very serious problem," 23 percent saw it as a "fairly serious problem," 5 percent as "not serious," and 14 percent had no opinion. In July, 1988, by a margin of 25 to 65 percent (10 percent had no opinion), a sampling disapproved of the way that President Reagan was handling the deficit problem. *The Gallup Report,* July 1988, p. 27.

12. *Business Week,* February 1, 1988, pp. 59–63. The quotation from Secretary Baker is on p. 61. See also Benjamin Friedman, *Day of Reckoning* (Random House, 1988), pp. 57–59 et passim.

13. Felix Rohatyn, *New York Review of Books,* February 18, 1988, p. 9.

14. *New York Times,* July 20, 1988, p. D1.

15. Robert J. Gordon, *Macroeconomics,* fourth edition (Little, Brown, 1987), p. 532. For the 1988 figure, see Rothschild, *New York Review of Books,* July 21, 1988, p. 33.

16. Rohatyn, *New York Review of Books,* February 18, 1988, p. 9.

CHAPTER 4

1. *Congressional Record,* U.S. Senate, January 5, 1951, pp. 55, 57.

2. Arthur H. Vandenberg, Jr., ed., *The Private Papers of Senator Vandenberg* (Houghton Mifflin, 1952), p. 569. Even if Senator Taft had opposed Truman on such a resolution, it would doubtless have passed by a wide margin. As Arthur Schlesinger, Jr., points out, "Few wars are unpopular in their first thirty days." *The Imperial Presidency* (Houghton Mifflin, Co., 1973), p. 135.

3. Vandenberg, *Private Papers,* pp. 570 and 572.

4. *Missouri vs. Holland* (1920) held that a treaty with Britain covering migratory birds was controlling over state legislation. *U.S. vs. Belmont* (1937) held that the executive agreement in 1933 recognizing the Soviet government carried the force of law, because it was within the president's constitutional powers to extend diplomatic recognition to a foreign government. *U.S. vs. Pink* (1942) held that the agreement recognizing the Soviet Union, by which the federal government assumed control over assets held by the state of New York, was supreme over state law.

5. Loch K. Johnson, *The Making of International Agreements: Congress Confronts the Executive* (New York University Press, 1984), pp. 87–89.

6. The Court ruled that the president could not, by executive agreement with Canada, supercede a statute regulating foreign commerce, since that power is given by the Constitution to Congress. See Louis Fisher, *President and Congress* (Free Press, 1972), pp. 45–46.

7. Quoted by Loch Johnson, *The Making of International Agreements,* p. 107.

8. "Transmittal of Executive Agreements to Congress," *Hearings,* Senate Report no. 92-591, 92nd Cong., 2nd Sess. (January, 1972), p. 3.

9. The speech was published as an op-ed in the *Wall Street Journal* on March 17, 1989.

10. Note, however, that President Kennedy did not involve any congressional leaders in these critical consultations. See Donald L. Robinson, *"To the Best of My Ability"* (W. W. Norton, 1987), p. 224n.

11. President Ford often complains that it is foolish to require that troops be withdrawn unless Congress positively affirms their involvement. As a former legislator himself, he knows how hard it is to patch together a positive vote in those chambers, regardless of the imperative.

12. P.L. 98–473 (1984). Executive Order 12333, dated December 4, 1981, states that the NSC "shall act as the highest executive branch entity that provides review of, guidance for, and direction to the conduct of all national foreign intelligence. . . ." During the Iran-contra hearings, the Reagan administration claimed that the Boland Amendment did not apply to the NSC staff. By its terms, it certainly did. Only by invocation of the president's own constitutional powers could the NSC staff have been insulated from this law.

13. In addition, Congress barred the State Department from making arrangements with other countries to support the contras in exchange for American foreign aid. *New York Times,* March 4, 1988, p. A4.

14. *Report of the Congressional Committees Investigating the Iran-Contra Affair,* 100 Cong., 1st Sess. (1987), H. Rept. 100–433; S. Rept. 100-216, pp. 3–4.

CHAPTER 5

1. This phrase is taken from a letter by Thomas Jefferson to Samuel Kercheval, July 12, 1816. It is part of Jefferson's call for a willingness to adjust institutions to "the progress of the human mind."

2. The framers were not, of course, advocates of novelty for its own sake, and they warned specifically against frequent alterations in the basic framework of government. (Beyond that, they were skeptical of the ability of the people at large to decide complicated public questions correctly.) In *The Federalist,* number 49, James Madison defends the Constitution's procedures for amendment against Jefferson's preference for a more facile method. He argues that Jefferson's approach (outlined in *Notes on the State of Virginia*) "would deprive the government of that veneration which time bestows on everything, and without which perhaps the wisest and freest governments would not possess the requisite stability." But there is no indication that the authors of *The Federalist* meant to choke off consideration of structural amendments. Indeed, in number 85, Hamilton specifically admits the possibility of "useful" amendments "applicable to the organization of the government."

3. "Party Government Under the Constitution," in Donald L. Robinson, editor, *Reforming American Government* (Westview Press, 1985), p. 99.

4. *Ibid.,* p. 94.

5. *Ibid.,* p. 96.

6. Reproduced from Lloyd N. Cutler and C. Douglas Dillon, "A Rebuttal to Arthur Schlesinger, Jr.," in Robinson, *Reforming American Government,* p. 56.

7. C. Douglas Dillon, "The Challenge of Modern Governance," in Robinson, *Reforming American Government,* p. 28.

8. *Ibid.,* p. 29.

9. James MacGregor Burns emphasizes and brilliantly illustrates this point in his magisterial new history of the "The American Experiment." See volume one, entitled *The Vineyard of Liberty* (Knopf, 1982), chapter 2.

CHAPTER 6

1. An eloquent reminder of these struggles came in the address by Justice Thurgood Marshall, in commemoration of the bicentennial of the Constitution, reported in *New York Times,* May 21, 1987, p. A22 and June 6, 1987, p. A22.

2. For a subtle analysis of this tradition of reverence for the Constitution, see Michael Kammen, *The Machine That Would Go of Itself* (Alfred A. Knopf, 1986).

3. Most American defenders of the Constitution are quite willing to acknowledge that the constitutional framework which works so well for us may not be universally applicable. Indeed, in warning against indiscriminate borrowing from other systems (such as Britain's), they stress the bond between culture and constitutional form. They are therefore not troubled to be reminded that few foreign countries have successfully copied our system of separated powers.

In fact, most of those who have tried to borrow from the United States—usually to get a stronger, more independent presidency—have come to grief rather quickly. See Fred Riggs, *The American Constitution: A Comparativist's Perspective* (unpublished manuscript, November, 1987). On the other hand, the French Fifth Republic, with its strong, separately elected president, is sometimes cited as an example of successful borrowing from the United States. See James W. Ceaser, "In Defense of the Separation of Powers," in *Separation of Powers: Does It Still Work?* (American Enterprise Institute, 1986), p. 191, where Ceaser cites William Safran, *The French Polity* (New York: David McKay, 1977), pp. 50–59.

4. Clinton Rossiter, *Constitutional Dictatorship* (Harcourt Brace, 1963), pp. 297–306 et passim.

5. James Q. Wilson, "Does the Separation of Powers Still Work?" *The Public Interest,* number 86 (Winter, 1987), p. 45. This issue also contains valuable interpretations of the Constitution's strength by Daniel Patrick Moynihan, Harvey C. Mansfield, Jr., Thomas Prangle and Michael J. Malbin, among others, presented on the 200th anniversary of its framing.

6. Quoted by Arthur M. Schlesinger, Jr., *Cycles of American History* (Houghton Mifflin, 1986), p. 311.

7. See Abraham D. Sofaer, *War, Foreign Affairs, and Constitutional Power* (Ballinger, 1976).

8. For a report on a poll finding enduring racism in America, see *New York Times,* August 9, 1988, p. A13.

9. Speech to the San Francisco Patent and Trademark Association, delivered in Maui, Hawaii, May 6, 1987. See also Glenn C. Loury's contribution to *The Public Interest,* "'Matters of Color'—Blacks and the Constitutional Order," Winter, 1987, pp. 109–123.

10. Thomas Byrne Edsall, *The New Politics of Inequality* (Norton, 1984), pp. 37–49.

11. *The Gallup Poll* (Scholarly Research, 1981), p. 171.

12. *Presidential Elections* (seventh edition) (Free Press, 1988), p. 254.

CHAPTER 7

1. The full text of this proposed amendment is printed in Donald L. Robinson, editor, *Reforming American Government* (Westview Press, 1985), p. 175.

2. "The Root of Republican Government: Terms of Office in the Legislative Branch," a pamphlet published by the Jefferson Foundation (1984), p. 1.

3. James L. Sundquist, *Constitutional Reform and Effective Government* (The Brookings Institution, 1986), p. 50.

4. *Ibid.,* p. 107.

5. So, at any rate, one often hears. See, e.g., Michael J. Malbin, in "Factions and Incentives in Congress," *The Public Interest* (Winter, 1987), pp. 91–108. But is it true? I can find no evidence in Max Farrand's *Records of the Federal Convention of 1787* or in *The Federalist* to support the claim that the framers established staggered elections specifically with the intent to diffuse political passions.

6. Sundquist, *Constitutional Reform,* p. 113.

7. For examples, see the third and fourth reforms outlined in this chapter.

8. For the text of such a statute, see Robinson, ed., *Reforming American Government,* pp. 119–120.

9. For the text of such a constitutional amendment, see Robinson, ed., *Reforming American Government,* pp. 177–178.

10. See Sundquist, *Constitutional Reform,* p. 85.

11. *Ibid.,* pp. 76–77, citing Norman Ornstein and others, *Vital Statistics on Congress, 1984-1985* (AEI, 1984), pp. 32–35.

12. Ornstein et al., *Vital Statistics on Congress, 1984-1985,* pp. 49–50.

13. Sundquist, *Constitutional Reform,* pp. 94–95.

14. *Ibid.,* p. 88.

15. For a different interpretation of data relating to ticket-splitting, see Martin Wattenberg, *The Decline of American Political Parties, 1952-1980* (Harvard University Press, 1984), pp. 17–23.

16. Richard M. Nixon, *RN: The Memoirs of Richard Nixon* (Grosset and Dunlap, 1978), p. 850.

17. James Sundquist, *The Decline and Resurgence of Congress* (Brookings, 1981), pp. 106–107, 273–293; also Sundquist, *Politics and Policy Under Eisen-*

hower, Kennedy and Johnson (Brookings, 1968), especially chapters IX and X.

18. See the evidence cited in the concluding section of chapter 2 of this book.

19. Sundquist, *Constitutional Reform*, p. 95.

20. *Ibid.*, p. 87.

21. Herbert Alexander, *Financing Politics*, third edition (CQ Press, 1984), p. 10.

22. David Butler, Howard Penniman, and Austin Ranney, eds., *Democracy at the Polls* (American Enterprise Institute, 1981), pp. 174–175.

23. Sundquist, *Constitutional Reform and Effective Government*, p. 200.

24. Ken Godwin, in *One Billion Dollars of Influence* (Chatham House, 1988), tells how politicians use direct mailing and shows how mail from Members of Congress to constituents, using the franking privilege instead of ordinary postage, increases as election day approaches.

25. Max Farrand, ed., *Records of the Federal Convention of 1787* (New Haven, 1911, 1937), vol. 2, p. 29.

26. *Ibid.*, p. 29.

27. Donald L. Robinson, *"To the Best of My Ability"* (Norton, 1987), pp. 81–83.

28. Farrand, ed., *Records of the Federal Convention of 1787*, vol. 2, pp. 56–57.

29. This is the so-called Lodge-Gossett Amendment, named for its principal sponsors in 1950, Senator Henry Cabot Lodge, Jr. (Republican, Massachusetts) and Representative Ed Gossett (Democrat, Texas).

30. The judicial standard of "one person, one vote" was enunciated in the opinion of Justice William O. Douglas, writing for the Supreme Court in *Gray vs. Sanders*, 83 Sup. Ct. 801 (1963), striking down a Georgia law that provided for winner-take-all primaries in statewide and congressional elections.

31. In its brief, Delaware relied upon research later published in John F. Banzhaf III, "One Man, 3.312 Votes: A Mathematical Analysis of the Electoral College," *Villanova Law Review*, v. 13, Winter, 1968.

32. Cited in Austin Ranney, "What Constitutional Changes Do Americans Want?", in Robinson, *Reforming American Government*, p. 283.

33. Neil Pierce and Lawrence D. Longley, *The People's President: The Electoral College in American History and the Direct Vote Alternative*, revised edition (Yale University Press, 1981), p. 205.

34. *Ibid.*, pp. 11–12.

35. Edward S. Corwin, *The President: Office and Powers* (New York University Press, 1957), p. 54.

36. Arthur M. Schlesinger, Jr., *The Cycles of American History* (Houghton Mifflin, 1986), p. 345.

37. *Ibid.*, p. 342. Schlesinger's essay, entitled "The Future of the Vice Presidency", pp. 335–372, states his case for elimination of the office and is a treasury of information about its history.

38. Michael Nelson, "Choosing the Vice President," *PS: Political Science and Politics*, Fall, 1988, p. 866.

39. Schlesinger, *The Cycles of American History,* p. 351.

40. *Ibid.,* p. 350. On the recent growth of the "institutional vice-presidency," see Paul C. Light, *Vice-Presidential Power* (Johns Hopkins University Press, 1984).

CHAPTER 8

1. Max Farrand, ed., *The Records of the Federal Convention of 1787* (Yale University Press, 1911, 1937), vol. 1, p. 379. Debate on June 22, 1787.

2. Don K. Price, *America's Unwritten Constitution* (Harvard University Press, 1985).

3. Jeffrey K. Tulis, in *The Rhetorical Presidency* (Princeton, 1987), has clarified the history of live addresses by presidents before Congress. Washington and John Adams presented their annual addresses live and entertained congressional delegations that delivered "replies" to the presidential addresses, but Jefferson thought that such exchanges reflected an "English habit" and were suspiciously monarchical. "Jefferson's practice of sending all messages to Congress in writing remained the rule," writes Tulis (p. 56), "until Woodrow Wilson dramatically broke precedent with his appearances before Congress." But neither Wilson nor his successors resumed the original practice of engaging in a formal exchange with congressional leaders at the beginning of the session.

4. *Congressional Quarterly Weekly Report,* October 5, 1974, p. 2682.

5. Philip B. Kurland and Ralph Lerner, eds., *The Founders' Constitution* (University of Chicago Press, 1987), Section 866; vol. 2, p. 373.

6. James L. Sundquist, *Constitutional Reform and Effective Government* (Brookings, 1986), p. 50.

7. Wilson's ideas on this subject were set forth most fully in an article published in *The International Review* in August, 1879. Excerpts are printed in Donald L. Robinson, ed., *Reforming American Government* (Westview Press, 1985), pp. 131–134.

8. Sundquist, *Constitutional Reform,* p. 51.

9. Hedrick Smith, *The Power Game* (Random House, 1988), pp. 713–714.

10. Wilson's leading biographer, Arthur S. Link, has written that the president, after his stroke, "for the balance of his term . . . remained a sick man, his physical constitution, psyche, and sense of reality shattered. He continued to function on a low level, but he could sit up or concentrate upon a subject for only short periods. He also suffered from severe changes in mood and from some paranoia. Consequently, Wilson was incapable of giving leadership to his party, to Congress, and to the people during one of the most critical periods in American history." "Woodrow Wilson," in Henry Graff, ed., *The Presidents: A Reference History* (Charles Scribner's Sons, 1984), p. 460. John D. Feerick also discusses the effects of Wilson's illness in his book *From Failing Hands* (Fordham University Press, 1965).

11. In Lincoln's case, he raised troops and directed that funds to pay for them be taken from the public treasury *before* Congress convened in 1861. According to Clinton Rossiter, this was the classic American case of "consti-

tutional dictatorship." See *Constitutional Dictatorship: Crisis Government in the Modern Democracies* (Harcourt, Brace and World, 1948, 1963), chapter XV.

12. "Of the more than 125 violent encounters in which the United States has been engaged, only five have involved a declaration of war." Cecil V. Crabb, Jr., and Pat M. Holt, *Invitation to Struggle: Congress, The President, and Foreign Policy* (CQ Press, 1989), p. 52.

13. See the preface, by Arthur Schlesinger, Jr., to Abraham Sofaer, *War, Foreign Affairs, and Constitutional Power* (Ballinger, 1976). For detailed evidence, see Sofaer's book, passim, and its sequel: Henry B. Cox, *War, Foreign Affairs, and Constitutional Power, 1829–1901* (Ballinger, 1984).

14. See Arthur M. Schlesinger, Jr., *The Imperial Presidency* (Houghton Mifflin, 1973), pp. 21–29, for other citations bearing on the insistence of the framers that the war powers be shared between president and Congress; also, David Adler's admirable summary of the evidence on this point, in "The Constitution and Presidential Warmaking," *Political Science Quarterly* (Spring, 1988).

15. Roy P. Basler, ed., *Collected Works of Lincoln* (Rutgers University Press, 1953), vol. I, pp. 451–452. The emphasis in the quotation is Lincoln's.

16. For an analysis of judicial responses to the undeclared war in Vietnam, see Schlesinger, *Imperial Presidency,* pp. 287–295; Donald L. Robinson, *"To the Best of My Ability"* (W. W. Norton, 1987), pp. 242–246; also, Christopher Pyle and Richard Pious, eds., *The President, Congress, and the Constitution* (Free Press, 1984), pp. 339–372, passim.

17. *Lowry vs. Reagan* 676 F. Supp. 333 (D.D.C., 1987).

18. Louis Fisher, *Constitutional Dialogues* (Princeton University Press, 1988), pp. 32–33, interpreting *Crockett vs. Reagan* (1982: 558 F.Supp 893, D.D.C.; 1984: cert. denied, 467 U.S. 1251). See also *Conyers vs. Reagan* (CA DC, 765 F.2d 1124), a vain attempt to have the Court decide issues relating to the invasion of Grenada.

19. See *The Federalist,* numbers 8 and 24–26, for Hamilton's discussion of standing armies.

20. James M. Buchanan and Richard E. Wagner, *Democracy in Deficit: The Political Legacy of Lord Keynes* (Academic Press, 1977).

21. Robert Eisner, *How Real Is the Federal Deficit?* (Free Press, 1986).

22. *Gallup Polls* 1982 (Scholarly Research, 1982), p. 125, and *Gallup Polls* 1987 (Scholarly Research, 1987), p. 184.

23. David Stockman, *The Triumph of Politics* (Harper & Row, 1986), p. 394.

CHAPTER 9

1. For a thoughtful assessment of these and other modes of calling elections out of the regular cycle, see James L. Sundquist, *Constitutional Reform and Effective Government* (Brookings, 1986), pp. 144–151. For the text of an amendment for dissolution based on a finding of no confidence, see Donald

L. Robinson, ed., *Reforming American Government* (Westview Press, 1985), pp. 254–257.

2. Joseph LaPalombara, *Democracy, Italian Style* (Yale University Press, 1987), p. 127.

3. Dillon's speech is printed in Robinson, ed., *Reforming American Government*, pp. 24–29. For a discussion of several reformist arguments that borrow from the parliamentary model, see Sundquist, *Constitutional Reform and Effective Government*, pp. 14–15 and 68–73.

4. Sundquist, *Constitutional Reform*, p. 162.

5. *Ibid.*, pp. 138–139. Sundquist identifies "five categories of circumstances in which a president would lose his capacity to lead the country yet could not be removed from office under the Constitution." They include: a pattern of criminal conduct that stems from the Oval Office but cannot be traced to the president personally; a pattern of abuse of power which, however egregious, does not violate a criminal statute to the satisfaction of one-third plus one of the Senate; a mental or emotional breakdown that is not clear enough to lead to removal by the Twenty-fifth Amendment; a general and irremediable loss of public confidence in the president, as in Herbert Hoover's case; and a deadlock between the executive and legislative branches so severe as to cripple the capacity of the government to cope with crisis.

6. David Butler and Austin Ranney, eds., *Referendums* (American Enterprise Institute, 1978), p. 67. Much of the information in this section is drawn from this admirable book, which presents analyses of the use of referendums in Switzerland (where they are used extensively), Australia, France and the United Kingdom, as well as in California. I regret that a new book by Thomas E. Cronin, *Direct Democracy: The Politics of Initiative, Referendum, and Recall* (Harvard University Press, 1989), was not available in time for me to use it in preparing this section.

7. Butler and Ranney, *Referendums*, pp. 12 and 17.

8. *Ibid.*, pp. 13 and 213–216.

9. *Ibid.*, pp. 69–73.

10. *Ibid.*, pp. 76–80.

11. *Ibid.*, pp. 82–85.

12. *Ibid.*, pp. 75–76.

13. *Ibid.*, p. 20.

14. Ernest Barker, *Reflections on Government* (Oxford University Press, 1942), p. 67; quoted in Butler and Ranney, *Referendums*, p. 35.

CHAPTER 10

1. For a careful analysis of these issues, see Louis Fisher, *Constitutional Conflicts Between Congress and the President* (Princeton University Press, 1985), chapter 8.

CHAPTER 11

1. *Mandate for Change* (Democratic National Committee, 1970), p. 15.

2. Statement before the Senate, September 5, 1979. *Congressional Record,* vol. 125, part 18, p. 22917, col. 3.

3. Dellinger's testimony was given on November 29, 1979, before the Subcommittee on the Constitution of the United States Senate's Committee on the Judiciary. For a full presentation of Dellinger's views, see his essay, "The Recurring Question of the 'Limited' Constitutional Convention," *Yale Law Journal,* vol. 88 (1979), 1632–1640. For the argument in favor of controls by statutes and judicial review, see Lawrence H. Tribe, "Issues Raised by Requesting Congress to Call a Constitutional Convention To Propose a Balanced Budget Amendment," *Pacific Law Journal,* July 1979, 627–640.

4. *Washington Post,* February 13, 1984; quoted in "To Make and To Alter Their Constitutions of Government" (Washington: The Jefferson Foundation, 1984), p. 12.

5. Note, too, that Lincoln, near the end of his First Inaugural Address, states a preference in principle for the convention method of constitutional amendment, on the ground that the other method only permits the people in the states to "take or reject propositions" originated by others; better, he thought, to "allow amendments to originate with the people themselves. . . ."

6. Quoted in "To Make and To Alter Their Constitutions of Government," p. 12.

APPENDIX

1. Amended by Section 2 of the Fourteenth Amendment.
2. The Seventeenth Amendment.
3. The Seventeenth Amendment.
4. Section 2 of the Twentieth Amendment.
5. The Sixteenth Amendment.
6. The Twelfth Amendment.
7. The Twenty-Fifth Amendment.
8. The Eleventh Amendment.
9. The Eleventh Amendment.
10. The Thirteenth Amendment.
11. Section 3 of the Twentieth Amendment.

Suggestions for Further Reading

The purpose of this brief essay is to call attention to published works that contribute to the assessment of the American constitutional system as we approach the twenty-first century. In the Notes section of this book, we cite sources on particular topics; this essay will highlight more general sources and studies.

The first job of those who wish to consider whether the American constitutional system needs reforming is to understand the existing document; the first book to study for that purpose is *The Federalist,* by Alexander Hamilton, James Madison, and John Jay.

Though there has been little hesitation, beginning with the Progressive period, to criticize the Federal Convention and assail the framers' motives, until recently there have been remarkably few studies which offered critical analyses of the structure of government established by the Constitution. One exception is Woodrow Wilson's *Congressional Government* (Johns Hopkins, 1981). Originally published in 1885 during the heyday of congressional power, it is no longer descriptively accurate, but it is powerfully written and still suggestive.

Even during the twentieth century, only a handful of books have set forth full-blown plans for constitutional revision. William MacDonald, in *A New Constitution for America* (B. W. Huebsch, 1921), proposed to center the government on a cabinet made up of legislators, reducing the president to a ceremonial head-of-state. MacDonald's model was squarely based on the British parliamentary system. William Yandell Elliott, a Harvard professor, in *The Need for Constitutional Reform* (Whittlesey House, 1935), reflected a desire, as the New Deal began to take shape, to facilitate national planning by strengthening the constitutional position of the executive. Henry Hazlitt, a conservative journalist, argued in *A New Constitution Now* (Whittlesey House, 1942), that the exigencies of war demanded a parliamentary form of government. Thomas K. Finletter, serving at the time as assistant secretary of state, in *Can Representative Government Do the Job?* (Reynal and Hitchcock, 1945), wrote that the post-war era would require unified government, best attained by coordinated terms, a joint executive-legislative council, and the possibility of presidential dissolution.

The 1970s saw two book-length proposals for constitutional revision: Charles Hardin's *Presidential Power and Accountability* (University of Chicago Press, 1974) and Rexford G. Tugwell's *The Emerging Constitution* (Harper's Magazine Press, 1974).

Many who considered constitutional revision have come to the conclusion that it would be a mistake. Among those who take the idea seriously before rejecting it are Harold Laski, *The American Presidency* (Harper and Brothers, 1940); Bob Eckhardt and Charles L. Black, Jr., *The Tides of Power* (Yale University Press, 1976); and Don K. Price, *America's Unwritten Constitution* (Harvard University Press, 1985).

The strains of the Vietnam War (1964–1973) and the Watergate scandal (1972–1974) stimulated new concerns about the American political system. The governance affecting Vietnam is analyzed by Leslie H. Gelb and Richard Betts, in *The Irony of Vietnam: The System Worked* (Brookings, 1979), and by Larry Berman, in *Planning a Tragedy: The Americanization of the War in Vietnam* (W. W. Norton, 1982). Pertinent summaries of Watergate are J. Anthony Lukas, *Nightmare: The Underside of the Nixon Years* (Penguin Books, 1976, 1988), Jonathan Schell, *The Time of Illusion* (Vintage, 1975), and Theodore H. White, *Breach of Faith: The Fall of Richard Nixon* (Atheneum, 1975).

Arthur M. Schlesinger, Jr., *The Imperial Presidency* (Houghton Mifflin, 1973, 1989), examines the constitutional strains produced by the preoccupation with national security. Richard P. Nathan, *The Plot That Failed: Nixon and the Administrative Presidency* (John Wiley, 1975), told how the effort to implement the New Federalism led to conflicts between the White House and the bureaucracy, weakening Nixon in his struggle to resist impeachment. Henry Reuss, then a member of Congress from Wisconsin, offered a plan for dissolution and new elections that was the subject of a symposium in 1974 at George Washington University. Papers delivered at that meeting were published in the university's *Law Review* (vol. 43, January, 1975).

Recent willingness to question the fitness of the American political system for the challenges of the twenty-first century owes much to the insight and courage of two men: C. Douglas Dillon and Lloyd N. Cutler. Dillon, an investment banker and former secretary of the treasury and under secretary of state, drew national press attention with a speech to the American Social Services Association in New York City in December, 1979, in which he declared that the system was not working to hold elected officials accountable for their performance in office. The following year, while still serving as counsel to President Carter, Cutler wrote "To Form a Government" (originally published in *Foreign Affairs,* Fall, 1980). In May, 1982, at Tufts University, Dillon gave a commencement address that reemphasized the themes of his earlier address and raised the thought that some of the difficulties being experienced by the government, both internally and in its foreign relations, were traceable to its antiquated structure.

The Committee on the Constitution System was founded in 1982 to carry on this inquiry into the fitness of our political system, and in early 1984,

Senator Nancy Landon Kassebaum joined Dillon and Cutler as co-chair. The following year, the Committee published a volume of "papers" devoted to the analysis of the system: Donald L. Robinson, ed., *Reforming American Government* (Westview Press, 1985). It included the texts of various proposed reforms, as well as articles and excerpts from books that addressed aspects of the argument for and against structural reforms. In January, 1987, the Committee published a 20-page pamphlet, entitled "A Bicentennial Analysis of the American Political Structure," containing a dozen suggestions for structural reform of the American system. (Copies of the pamphlet are available from the Committee at Suite 410, 1755 Massachusetts Avenue NW, Washington, DC 20036.)

Three scholars who have worked closely with the Committee on the Constitutional System have written book-length analyses of the need for structural reform of the American political system. James Sundquist, *Constitutional Reform and Effective Government* (Brookings, 1986), closely examines the whole range of proposals for breaking deadlocks and encouraging more effective, accountable government. James Burns, *The Power to Lead* (Simon & Schuster, 1984), concentrates on the need to strengthen parties. Charles Hardin directs his attention to the separation of powers, in *Constitutional Reform in the United States* (Iowa State University Press, forthcoming).

Also, in November, 1983, Henry Reuss, then chairman of the Joint Economic Committee of Congress and an active participant in CCS, conducted hearings on "Political Economy and Constitutional Reform." The two-volume report of those hearings (November–December, 1982; 97th Congress, 2d session) is a valuable collection of materials on the whole question of constitutional reform.

As the Committee's inquiries and positions became better known, critics have begun to respond. Notable among those who explicitly address the proposals of CCS are Arthur M. Schlesinger, Jr., "After the Imperial Presidency," in *Cycles of American History* (Houghton Mifflin, 1986); Everett Carll Ladd, *The American Polity,* second edition (W. W. Norton, 1987), pp. 304–318; Mark Petracca, "Remedies Worse Than the Disease: Founding Principles and Recent Proposals for Constitutional Reform," a paper delivered at the annual meeting of the American Political Science Association, Washington, DC, September, 1988; from a conservative viewpoint: James Q. Wilson, "Does the Separation of Powers Still Work?", in *The Public Interest* (Winter 1987); and James Ceaser, "In Defense of Separation of Powers," in Robert Goldwin and Art Kaufman, eds., *Separation of Powers: Does It Still Work?* (AEI, 1986), pp. 168–193; and, from a populist point of view: Jeanne Hahn, "NeoHamiltonianism: A Democratic Critique," in John F. Manley and Kenneth M. Dolbeare, eds., *The Case Against the Constitution: From the Antifederalists to the Present* (M. E. Sharpe, 1987), pp. 143–176. Burke Marshall, ed., *A Workable Government? The Constitution After 200 Years* (Norton, 1987), without mentioning the Committee's work explicitly, presents essays given at a conference which concluded that the Constitution's structure has proven sound and that "there is no fundamental reason to believe that it will not work as well for the closing years of this century, and into the next" (p. 236).

In addition to these works that deal directly with the concerns of this book, we ought to mention several recent publications that shed light on closely related themes. Some focus on the relation of Congress and the presidency. James Sundquist, *The Decline and Resurgence of Congress* (Brookings, 1981); Louis Fisher, *The Politics of Shared Power,* second edition (CQ Press, 1987); and Louis Fisher, *Constitutional Conflicts Between Congress and the President* (Princeton, 1985), trace the ebb and flow of power between the two branches through recent events. Arthur Maass, in *Congress and the Common Good* (Basic Books, 1983), presents an analysis based on the contention that Congress serves, not narrow special interests, but the "public interest" in its broadest sense. Hedrick Smith, in *The Power Game* (Random House, 1988), Part IV, examines recent experience with "divided government" in Washington and presents several reforms.

Other books concentrate on the presidency. Theodore Lowi, *The Personal President* (Cornell University Press, 1985), bewails the rise of the "plebiscitary presidency" and recommends a "more responsible multiparty system" and a "build-down" of the institutional presidency. Robert Shogan, *None of the Above: Why Presidents Fail, and What Can Be Done About It* (New American Library, 1982), is a vigorous critique by a journalist who watches the presidency closely. Three other books examine proposed reforms in the context of an overall analysis of the presidency: Larry Berman, *The New American Presidency* (Little, Brown, 1987); Thomas E. Cronin, *The State of the Presidency,* second edition (Little, Brown, 1980); and Donald L. Robinson, *"To the Best of My Ability": The Presidency and the Constitution* (W. W. Norton, 1987). Jeffrey K. Tulis, *The Rhetorical Presidency* (Princeton University Press, 1987), notes that twentieth-century presidents, turning their backs on the framers' intent and example, routinely appeal to the people "over the heads" of Congress, a development that has transformed the presidency and the conduct of American governance. Ralph Ketcham, *Presidents Above Party* (UNC Press, 1987), reinforces Tulis's point with a demonstration of the principled aloofness from partisan politics shown by the first six presidents.

Bert A. Rockman, *The Leadership Question* (Praeger, 1984), examines the difficulties that must be overcome in moving the government to effective action. David A. Stockman, *The Triumph of Politics: Why the Reagan Revolution Failed* (Harper & Row, 1986), makes a similar point in telling how Reagan piled up huge deficits. Edward R. Tufte, on the other hand, argues, in *Political Control of the Economy* (Princeton University Press, 1978), that "political life affects economic outcomes in a regular, persistent fashion."

The Iran-contra affair was the occasion for two useful reflections on the political system: *The Tower Commission Report* (New York Times/Bantam Books, 1987), prepared by John Tower, Edmund Muskie, Brent Scowcroft, focused mainly on the sale of arms to Iran and slighted the Nicaragua connection; *Veil* (Simon & Schuster, 1987), by Bob Woodward, recounted "the secret wars of the CIA, 1981-1987." Sadly, the affair itself was swamped by the presidential campaign of 1988 before its lessons could be drawn and acted upon.

The role of parties has been a preoccupation of many political scientists since World War II. The debate began with an analysis and program of reform, *Toward a More Responsible Two-Party System* (Rinehart, 1950), produced by the Committee on Political Parties of the American Political Science Association. For a critical study of this report, see Evron M. Kirkpatrick, " 'Toward a More Responsible Two-Party System': Political Science, Policy Science, or Pseudo-Science?" *American Political Science Review,* LXV (December 71), 965–990; for a more sympathetic analysis, Gerald Pomper, "Toward a More Responsible Two-Party System? What, Again?" *Journal of Politics,* vol. 33 (November 1971), 916–940.

James M. Burns, *The Deadlock of Democracy* (Prentice-Hall, 1963), traces the travail of the parties to its root in the constitutional structure. Thomas Edsall, in *The New Politics of Inequality* (Norton, 1985), presents a shrewd analysis of changes that have overtaken the party system since the mid-1970s, resulting in a politics that is less responsive to poorer voters. Martin Wattenberg, *The Decline of American Political Parties, 1952–1980* (Harvard Uuniversity Press, 1984), outlines evidence of the decline of political parties and traces it partly to the tendency of the public to "echo" the media's neglect of parties.

Among many works that deal with the effect of modern media on political life, two are particularly insightful: Austin Ranney, *Channels of Power: The Impact of Television on American Politics* (Basic Books, 1983), presents a discerning analysis of how elected officials have been weakened and the electoral process altered by television; and Martin Linsky, *Impact: How the Press Affects Federal Policymaking* (W. W. Norton, 1986).

Three recent collections of essays on trends and problems in American politics are especially valuable for those who wish to assess the system's performance. John E. Chubb and Paul Peterson, eds., *The New Direction in American Politics* (Brookings, 1985), contains papers on voters and elections, and on institutions and policy, including Samuel Kernell on the tensions between campaigning and governing in the contemporary Presidency; Thomas Cavanagh and James Sundquist on "The New Two-Party System," and Paul Peterson on "The New Politics of Deficits." A. James Reichley, ed., *Elections American Style* (Brookings, 1987), includes a valuable exchange between James Sundquist and Everett Carll Ladd on the need to reform the parties; also, Larry Sabato on campaign financing, and Walter Dean Burnham on "The Turnout Problem." Alexander Heard and Michael Nelson, eds., *Presidential Selection* (Duke University Press, 1987), has an essay on campaign finance by Xandra Kayden, one on television and presidential politics by Thomas Patterson (he recommends a generous allotment of television time to candidates during the last four weeks of campaign), and one by Ralf Dahrendorf on "Presidential Selection and Continuity in Foreign Policy."

Nelson W. Polsby, *Consequences of Party Reform* (Oxford University Press, 1983), analyzes the effect of reforms initiated in the aftermath of the 1968 conventions. Polsby and Aaron Wildavsky, in *Presidential Elections,* seventh edition (Free Press, 1988), discuss the pros and cons of such specific reforms as permanent voter enrollment and changes in the electoral college.

Recent years have seen the publication of many valuable studies of the constitutional tradition in America. Notable among these are Charles A. Lofgren, *"Government from Reflection and Choice": Constitutional Essays on War,*

Foreign Relations and Federalism (Oxford University Press, 1986); Michael Kammen, *The Machine That Would Go of Itself* (Knopf, 1986); Forrest McDonald, *Novus Ordo Seclorum: The Intellectual Origins of the Constitution* (University Press of Kansas, 1985); and Edmund S. Morgan, *Inventing the People: The Rise of Popular Sovereignty in England and America* (Norton, 1988).

The Jefferson Foundation seeks "to enhance the public's critical understanding of the Constitution . . . by involving citizens in debate and discussion of the fundamental principles of American government" and to study "constitutional reforms which have been endorsed by various groups as ways of improving the structure and functioning of government." To facilitate these discussions, the Foundation has produced pamphlets on such topics as terms of office, the executive veto, the amendment process, judicial independence, and the single, six-year term for presidents. Their address is The Jefferson Foundation, 1529 18th Street NW, Washington, DC 20036.

Finally, we offer a suggestion or two in the vast field of comparative constitutionalism. A good place to start is with Carl J. Friedrich, *The Impact of American Constitutionalism Abroad* (Holmes and Meier, 1967). Arend Lijphart, *Democracies: Patterns of Majoritarian and Consensus Government in Twenty-One Countries* (Yale, 1984), in a little over 200 closely reasoned and empirically rich pages, examines "twenty-one democracies [including the United States] that have been in existence for a long time [and] have developed quite different formal and informal institutions for translating citizen preferences into public policies." Lijphart's footnotes offer a survey of recent literature in political science that bears on constitutional form and practice. In August, 1988, Fred Riggs of the University of Hawaii organized a panel on "comparative presidentialism" at the congress of the International Political Science Association in Washington, DC. The panel heard presentations by Juan Linz of Yale on the general topic, Arturo Valenzuela of Georgetown University on the failure of presidentialism in Chile, Jonathan Hartlyn of the University of North Carolina on presidentialism in Colombian politics; and Professor Riggs on "The Survival of Presidentialism in America." Earlier, in September, 1987, Professor Linz presented a paper on "The United States Constitution Abroad: The Failure of Presidentialism," at the annual meeting of the American Political Science Association.

Board of Directors, Committee on the Constitutional System

Index